Really Easy Songs

T0079364

PLAYBACK+
Speed • Pitch • Balance • Loop

To access audio visit:
www.halleonard.com/mylibrary

Enter Code
5055-0978-0281-2875

ISBN 978-1-5400-0361-4

7777 W. BLUEMOUND RD. P.O. BOX 13819 MILWAUKEE, WI 53213

For all works contained herein:
Unauthorized copying, arranging, adapting, recording, Internet posting, public performance,
or other distribution of the printed or recorded music in this publication is an infringement of copyright.
Infringers are liable under the law.

Visit Hal Leonard Online at
www.halleonard.com

All the Small Things

Words and Music by Tom DeLonge, Travis Barker and Mark Hoppus

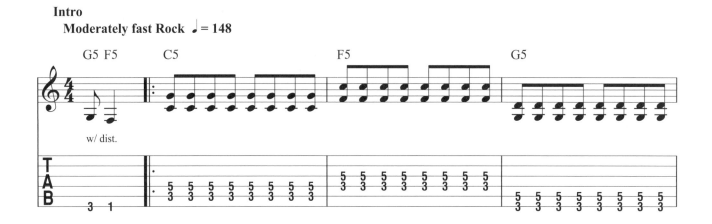

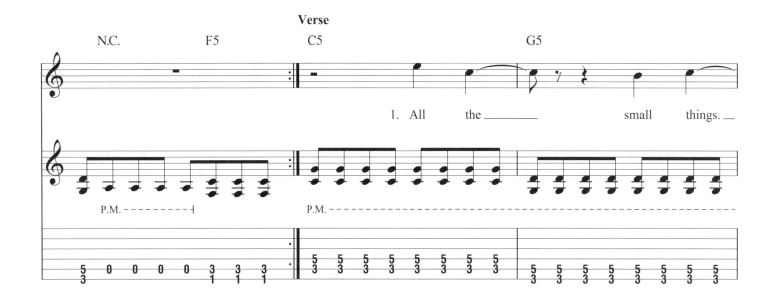

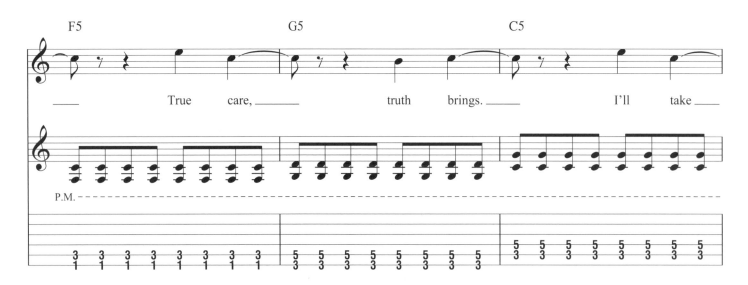

Copyright © 1999 EMI April Music Inc., Jolly Old Saint Dick, HMNIM Music and Beat Poet Music
All Rights on behalf of EMI April Music Inc. and Jolly Old Saint Dick Administered by
Sony/ATV Music Publishing LLC, 424 Church Street, Suite 1200, Nashville, TN 37219
All Rights on behalf of HMNIM Music and Beat Poet Music Administered by Kobalt Songs Music Publishing
International Copyright Secured   All Rights Reserved

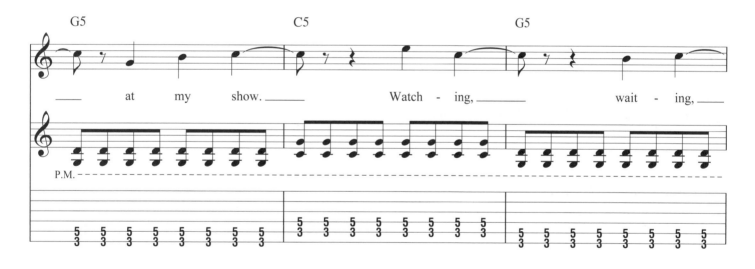

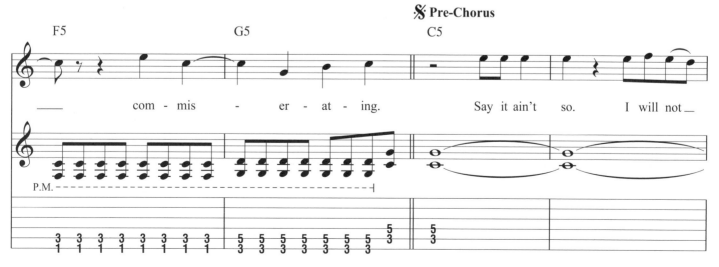

3

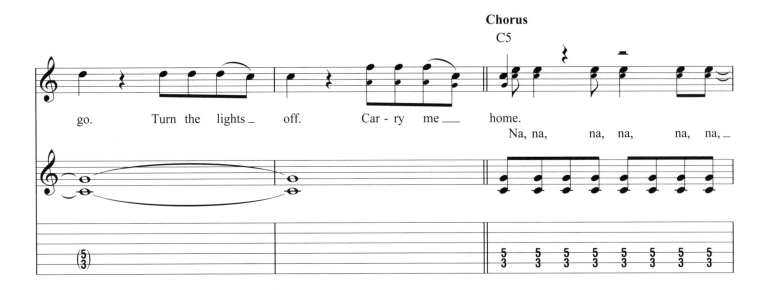

Chorus

go. Turn the lights _ off. Car - ry me _ home. Na, na, na, na, na, na, _

_ na, na, na, na. Na, na, na, na, na, na, _ na, na, na, na.

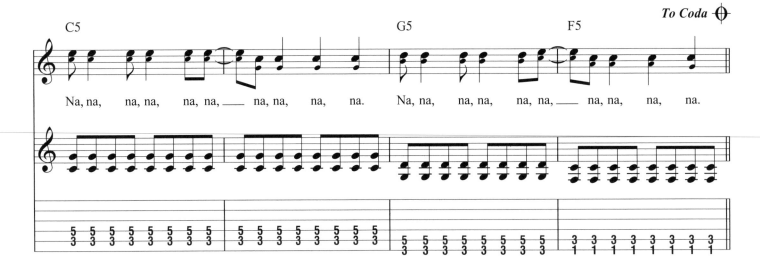

To Coda ⊕

Na, na, na, na, na, na, _ na, na, na, na. Na, na, na, na, na, na, _ na, na, na, na.

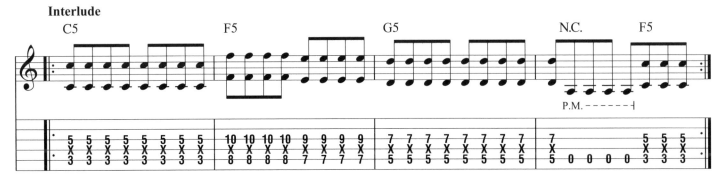

Interlude

P.M. - - - - - -

Verse

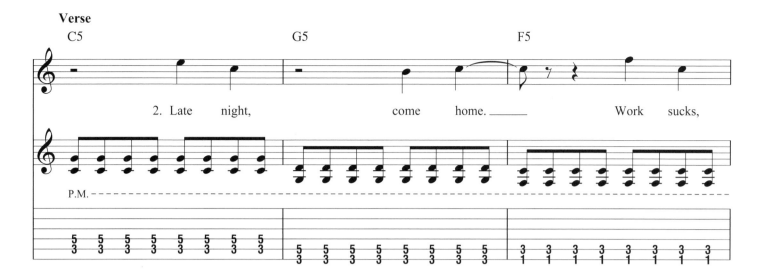

2. Late night, come home. _____ Work sucks,

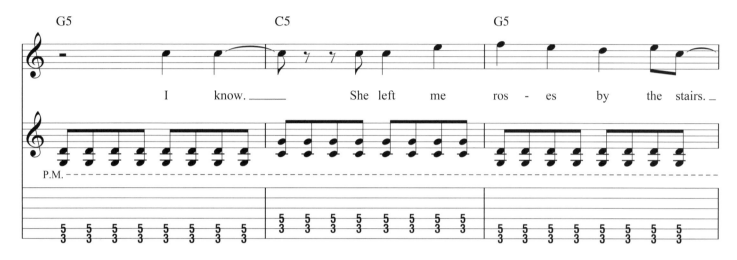

I know. _____ She left me ros - es by the stairs. _

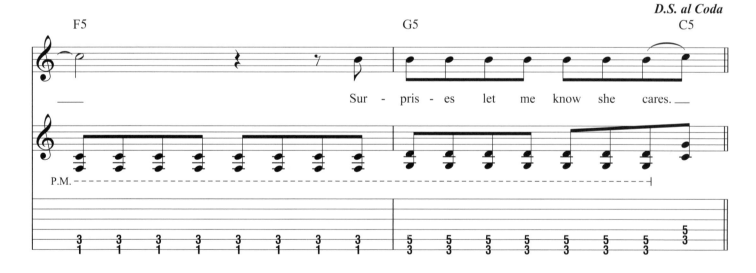

D.S. al Coda

Sur - pris - es let me know she cares. _

Coda
Interlude

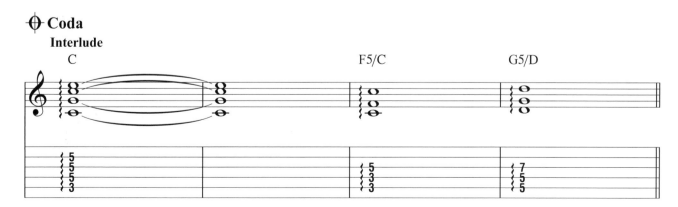

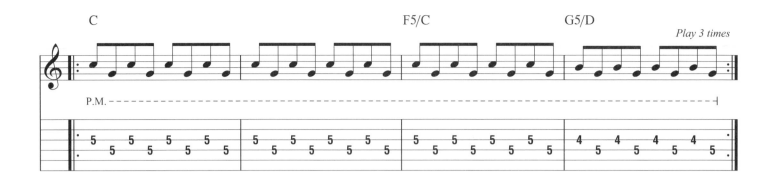

Outro

Say it ain't so. I will not ___ go. Turn the lights ___

off. Car - ry me ___ home. Keep your head still. I'll be your ___

thrill. The night will go ___ on, my lit - tle wind - mill. Say it ain't

(Na, na, na, na, na, na, ___

Brain Stew

Words by Billie Joe Armstrong
Music by Green Day

Tune down 1/2 step:
(low to high) Eb-Ab-Db-Gb-Bb-Eb

Intro
Moderately ♩ = 76

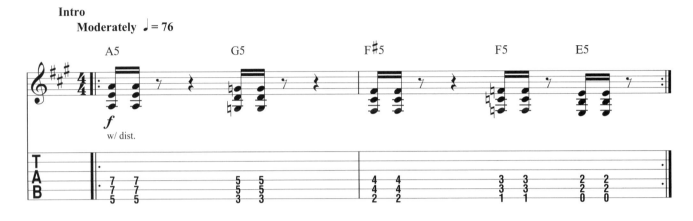

Verse

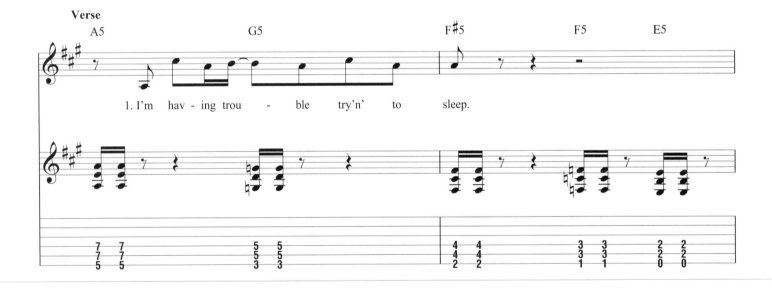

1. I'm hav-ing trou — ble try'n' to sleep.

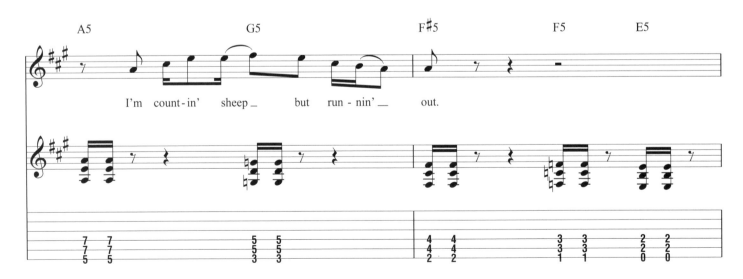

I'm count-in' sheep __ but run-nin' __ out.

© 1995, 1996 WB MUSIC CORP. and GREEN DAZE MUSIC
All Rights Administered by WB MUSIC CORP.
All Rights Reserved   Used by Permission

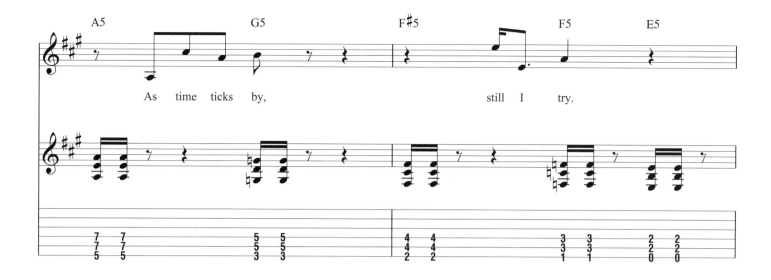

As time ticks by, still I try.

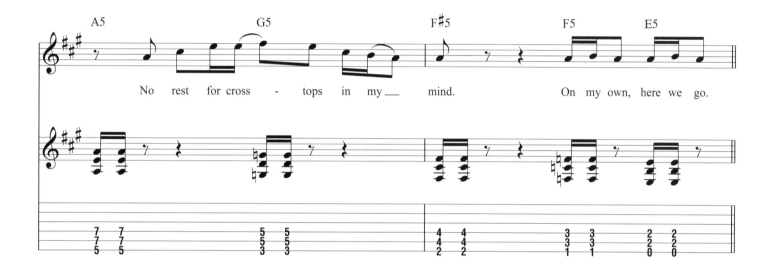

No rest for cross - tops in my ___ mind. On my own, here we go.

Interlude

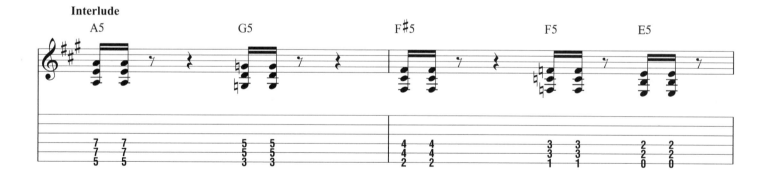

Interlude

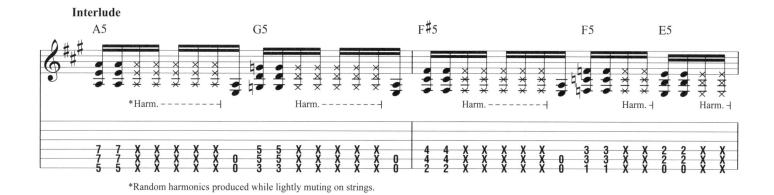

*Random harmonics produced while lightly muting on strings.

2nd time, D.S. al Coda

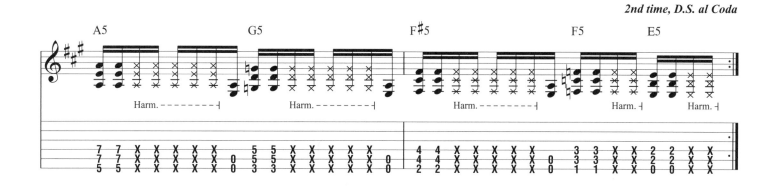

Coda

Outro

room.　　　On my own,　here we go.

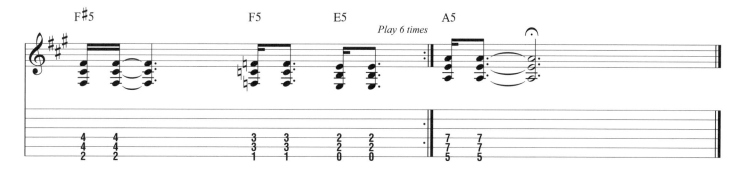

Additional Lyrics

3. My mind is set on overdrive.
　 The clock is laughing in my face.
　 Crooked spine, my senses dulled.
　 Passed the point of delerium.
　 On my own, here we go.

Californication

Words and Music by Anthony Kiedis, Flea, John Frusciante and Chad Smith

© 1999 MOEBETOBLAME MUSIC
All Rights Reserved   Used by Permission

Interlude

2. It's the

%Verse

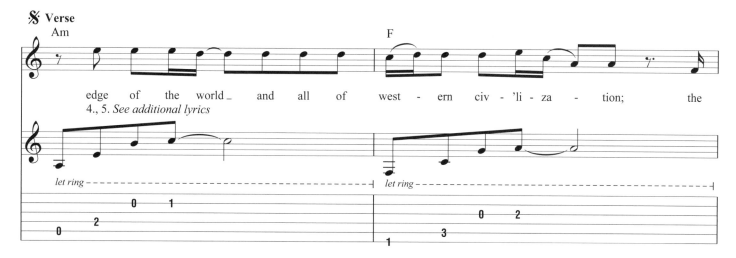

edge of the world _ and all of west - ern civ -'li - za - tion; the
4., 5. *See additional lyrics*

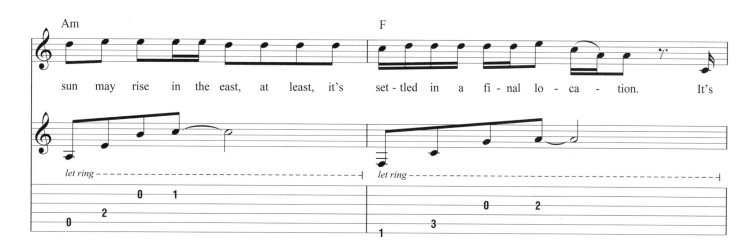

sun may rise in the east, at least, it's set - tled in a fi - nal lo - ca - tion. It's

Interlude

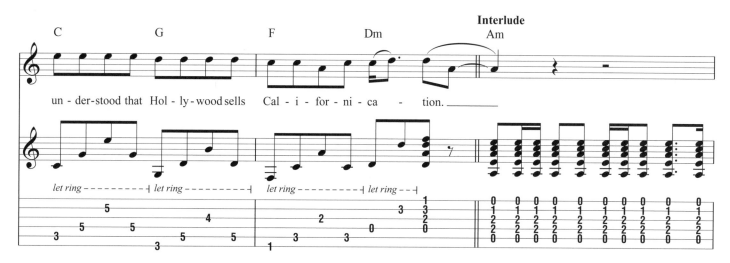

un - der-stood that Hol - ly-wood sells Cal - i - for - ni - ca - tion. _

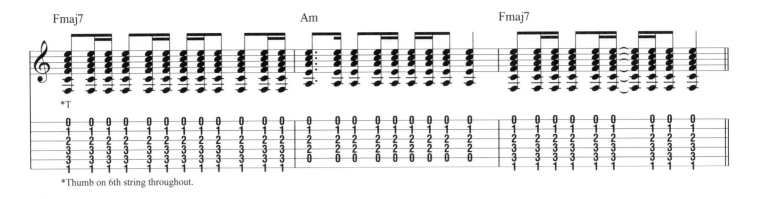

*Thumb on 6th string throughout.

Pre-Chorus

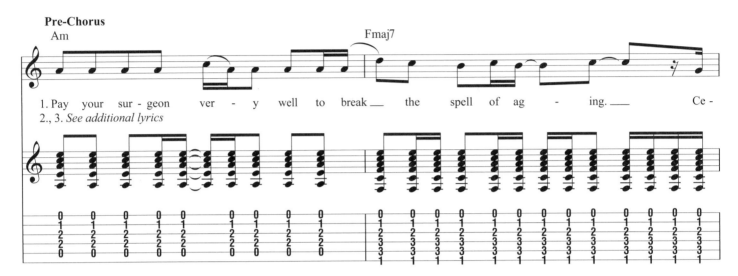

1. Pay your sur-geon ver-y well to break ___ the spell of ag ___ ing. ___ Ce-
2., 3. See additional lyrics

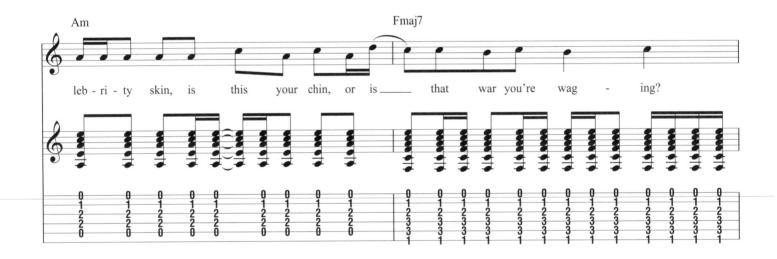

leb-ri-ty skin, is this your chin, or is ___ that war you're wag ___ ing?

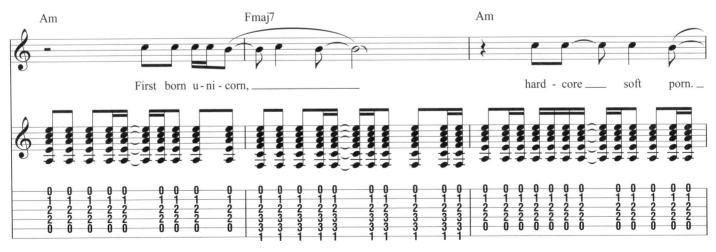

First born u-ni-corn, ___ hard-core ___ soft porn.

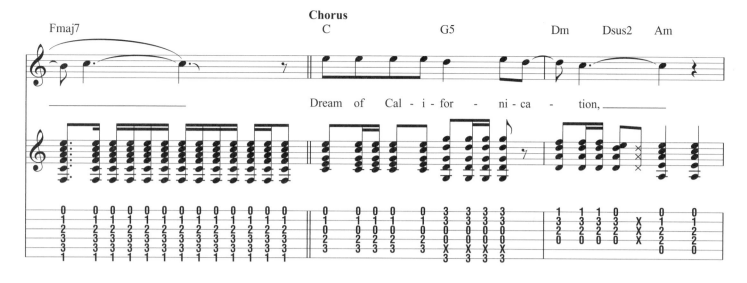

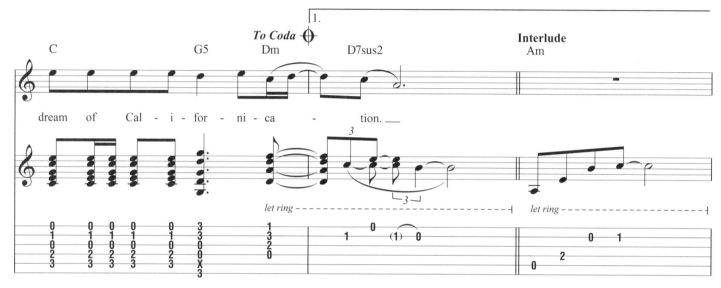

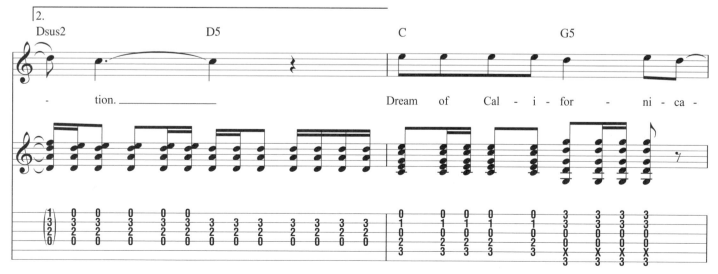

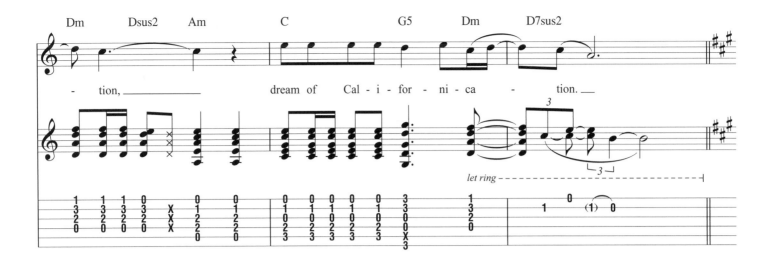

-tion,_____ dream of Cal - i - for - ni - ca - tion. _____

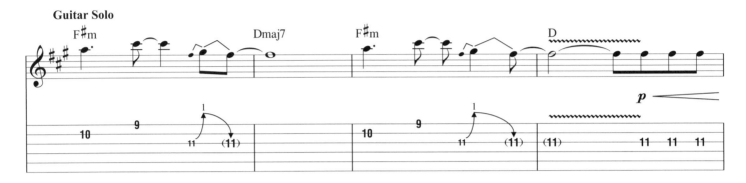

Guitar Solo

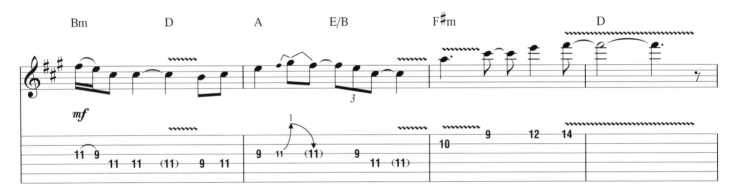

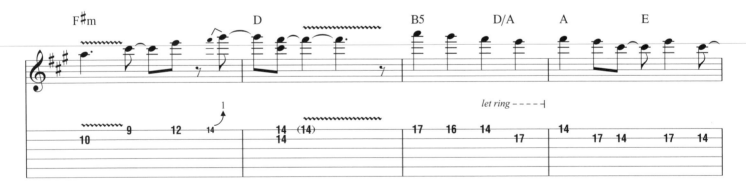

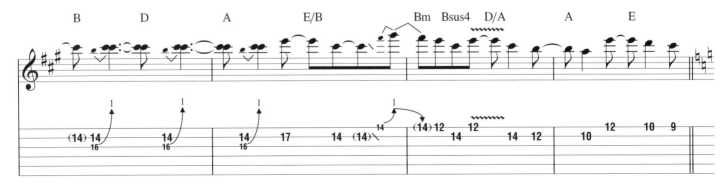

Interlude

D.S. al Coda

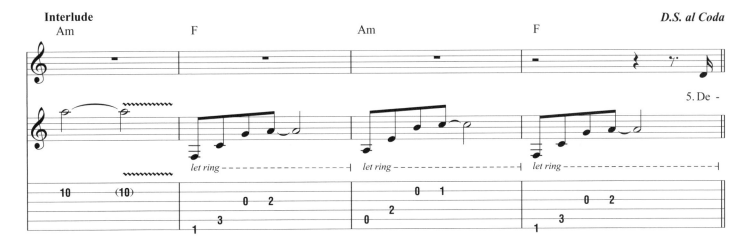

5. De -

⊕ Coda

- tion. _____ Dream of Cal - i - for - ni - ca - tion, _____

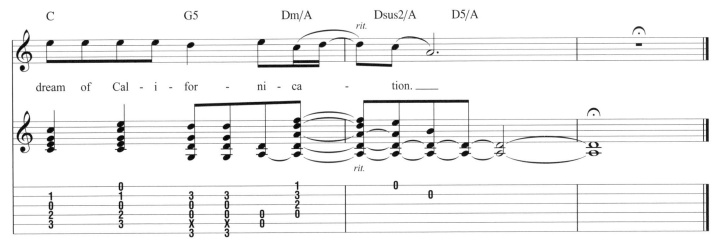

dream of Cal - i - for - ni - ca - tion. _____

Additional Lyrics

3. Marry me girl, be my fairy to the world,
   Be my very own constellation;
   A teenage bride with a baby inside
   Gettin' high on information.
   And buy me a star on the boulevard;
   It's Californication.

4. Space may be the final frontier
   But it's made in a Hollywood basement;
   Cobain can you hear the spheres
   Singing songs off station to station?
   And Alderon's not far away;
   It's Californication.

Pre-Chorus 2. Born and raised by those who praise control of population.
   Ev'rybody's been there and I don't mean on vacation.
   First born unicorn, hardcore soft porn.

5. Destruction leads to a very rough road
   But it also breeds creation;
   And earthquakes are to a girl's guitar,
   They're just another good vibration.
   And tidal waves couldn't save the world
   From Californication.

Pre-Chorus 3. Pay your surgeon very well to break the spell of aging.
   Sicker than the rest, there is no test, but this is what you're craving.
   First born unicorn, hardcore soft porn.

Free Fallin'

Words and Music by Tom Petty and Jeff Lynne

Capo I

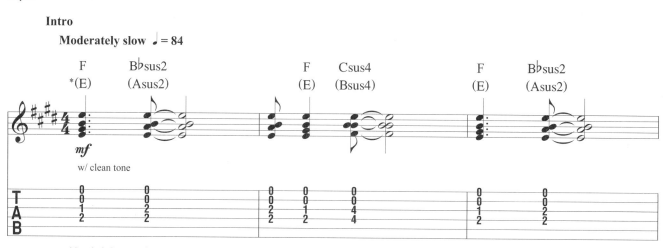

*Symbols in parentheses represent chord names respective to capoed guitar.
Symbols above reflect actual sounding chords. Capoed fret is "0" in tab.

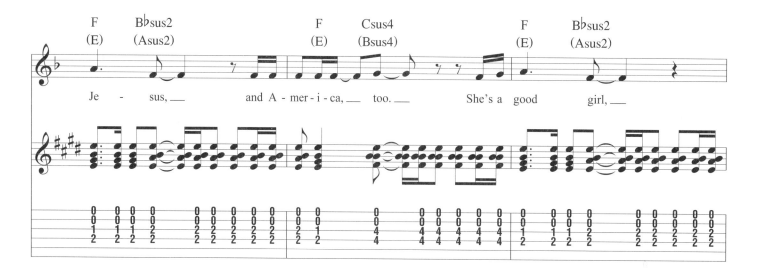

Copyright © 1989 Gone Gator Music and EMI April Music Inc.
All Rights for EMI April Music Inc. Administered by Sony/ATV Music Publishing LLC, 424 Church Street, Suite 1200, Nashville, TN 37219
All Rights Reserved   Used by Permission

cra-zy 'bout __ El - vis, loves hors - es ____ and her boy-friend, too. __

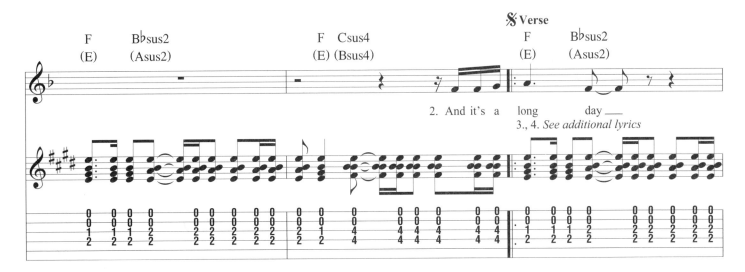

%Verse

2. And it's a long day __
3., 4. *See additional lyrics*

liv-in' in Re-se - da. There's a free - way __ run-nin' through the yard. __ And I'm a

bad boy __ 'cause I don't e - ven miss __ her. I'm a bad boy __ for

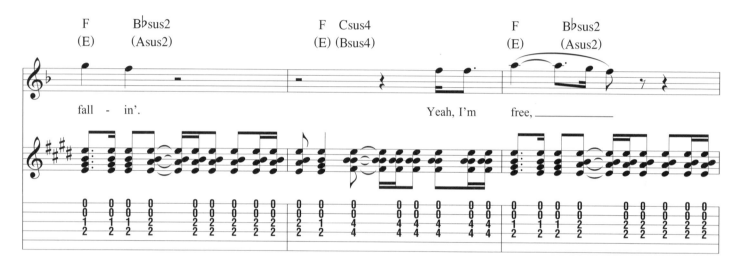

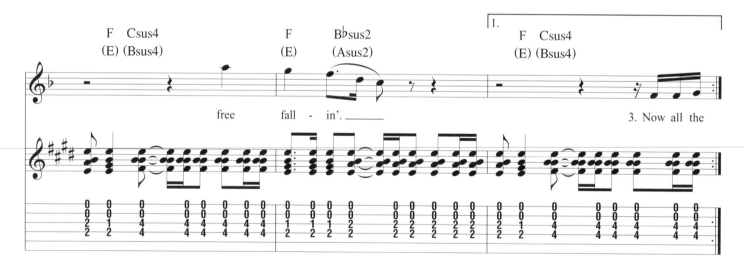

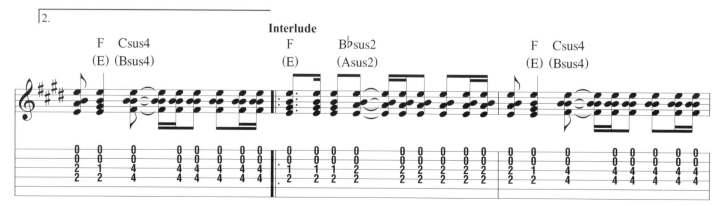

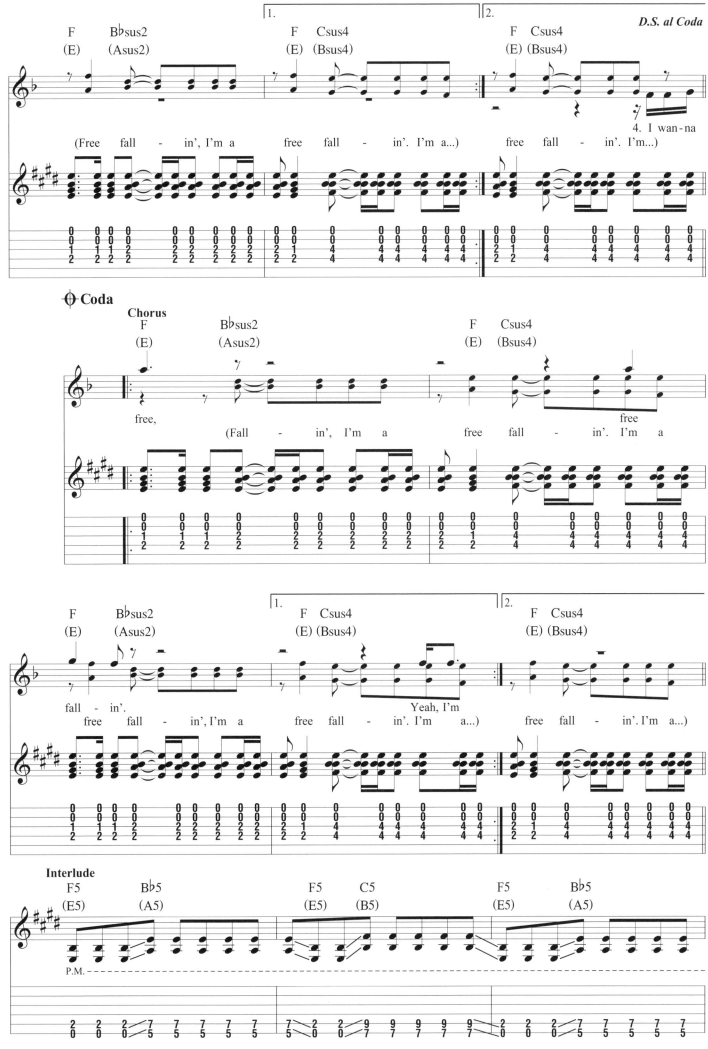

Outro-Chorus

Yeah, I'm free, _____ free

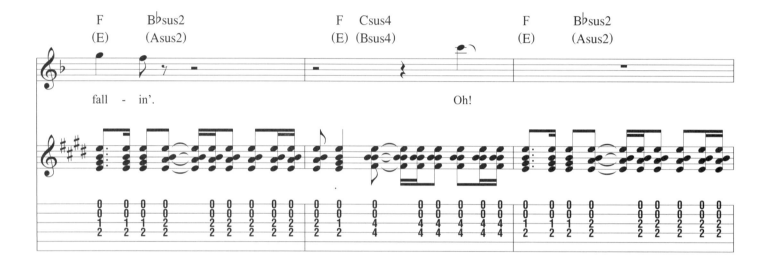

fall - in'.   Oh!

Repeat and fade

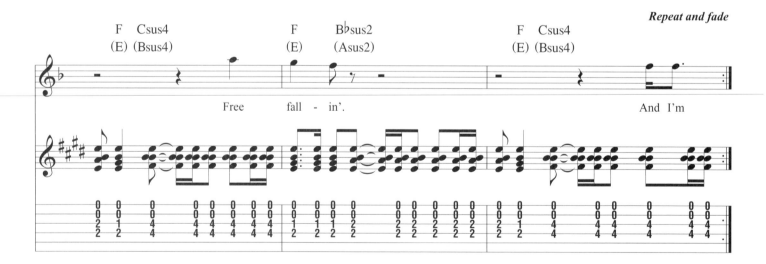

Free   fall - in'.   And I'm

Additional Lyrics

3. Now all the vampires walkin' through the valley
   Move west down Ventura Boulevard.
   And all the bad boys are standin' in the shadows,
   And the good girls are home with broken hearts.

4. I wanna glide down over Mulholland,
   I wanna write her name in the sky.
   I'm gonna free fall out into nothin',
   Gonna leave this world for a while.

Island in the Sun

Words and Music by Rivers Cuomo

Intro
Moderately ♩ = 118

Hip, hip.

w/ clean tone

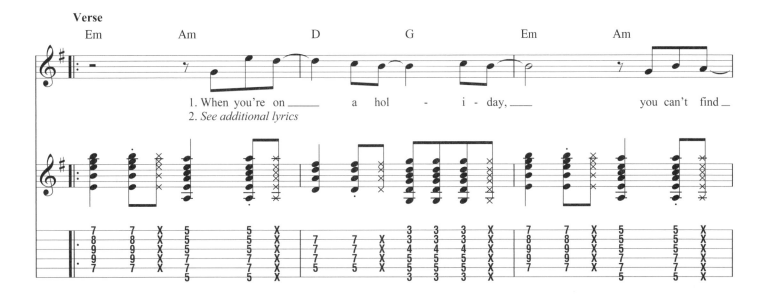

Verse

1. When you're on ___ a hol - i - day, ___ you can't find ___
2. *See additional lyrics*

___ no words ___ to say. ___ All the things ___ that come ___ to you, ___

Copyright © 2001 E.O. Smith Music
International Copyright Secured   All Rights Reserved

% Chorus

3rd time, substitute Fill 1

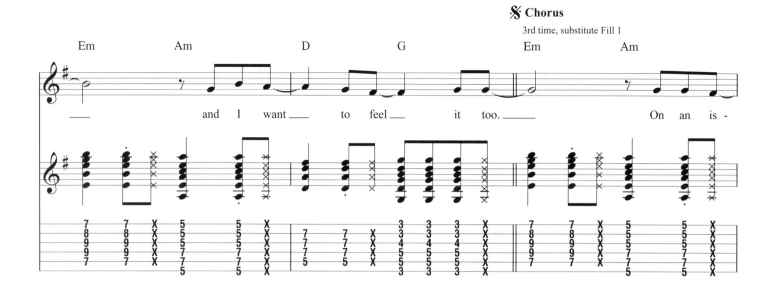

and I want to feel it too. On an is-

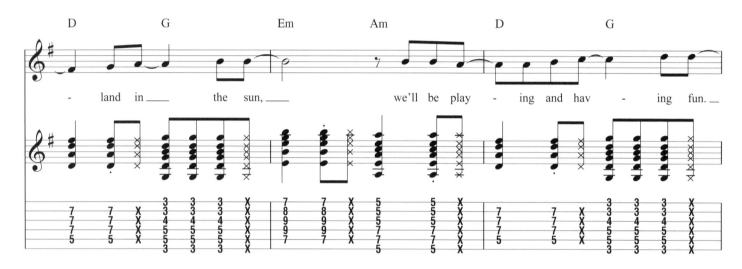

- land in the sun, we'll be play - ing and hav - ing fun.

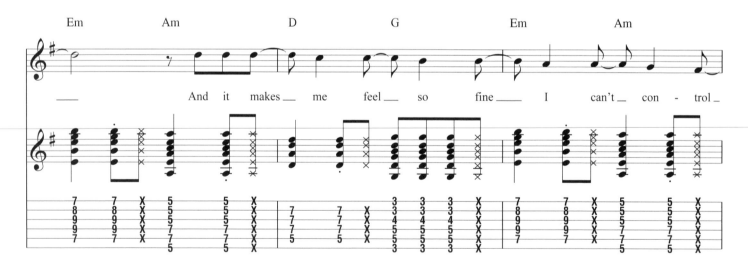

And it makes me feel so fine I can't con - trol

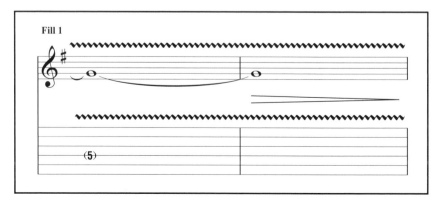

Fill 1

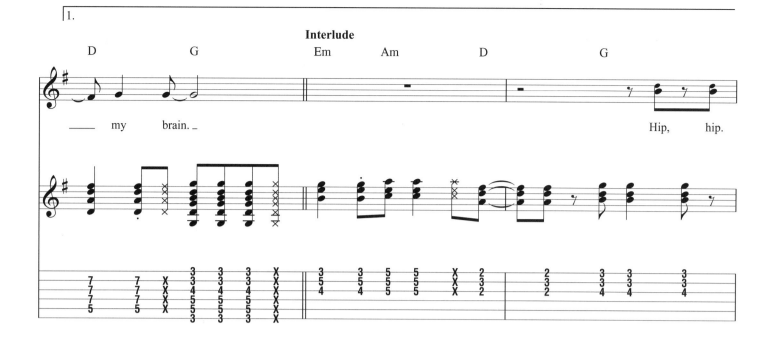

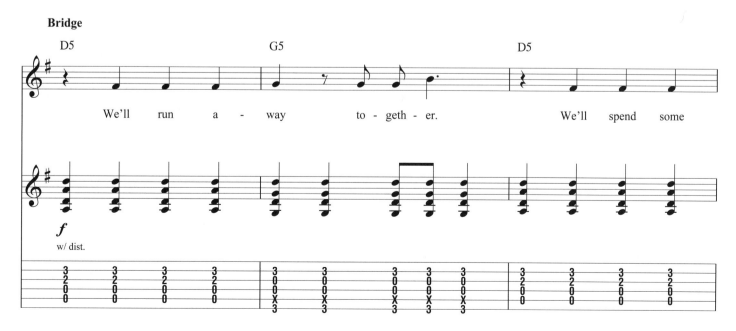

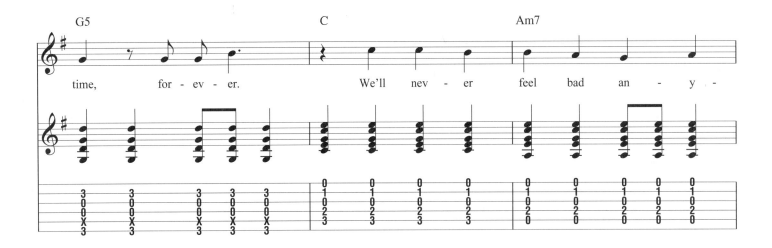

time, for - ev - er. We'll nev - er feel bad an - y -

To Coda ⊕

Interlude

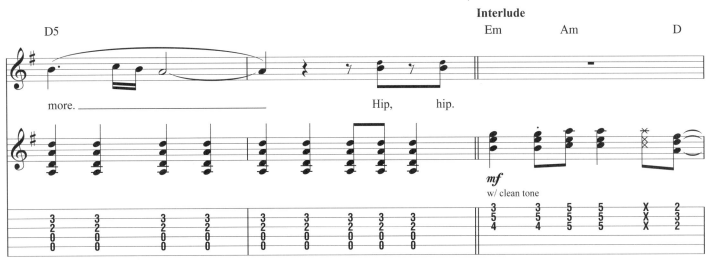

more. _____ Hip, hip.

mf
w/ clean tone

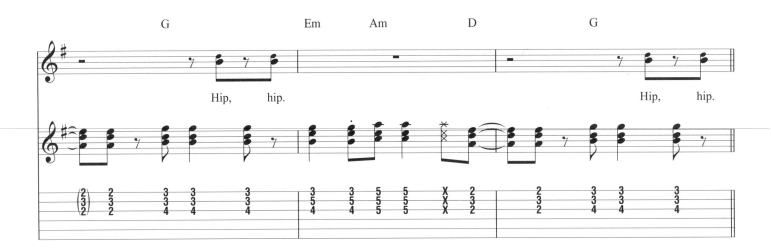

Hip, hip. Hip, hip.

Guitar Solo

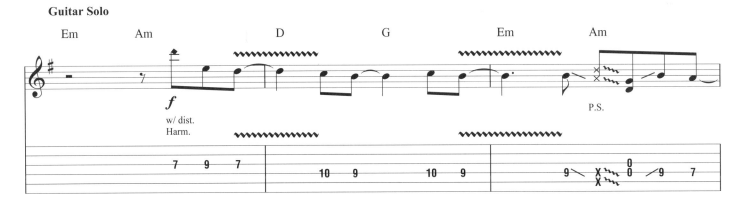

f
w/ dist.
Harm.

P.S.

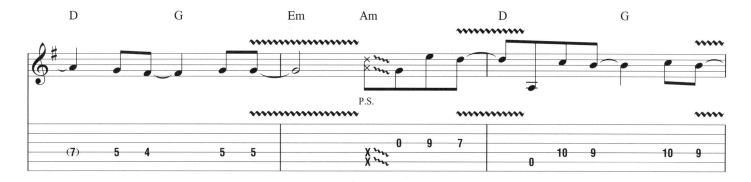

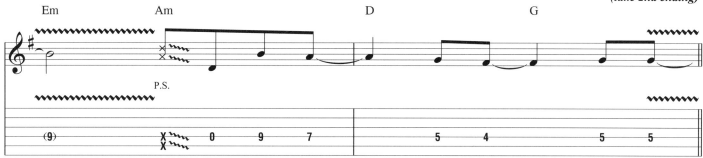

D.S. al Coda
(take 2nd ending)

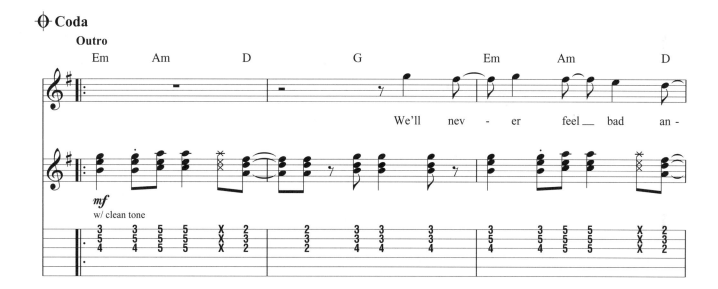

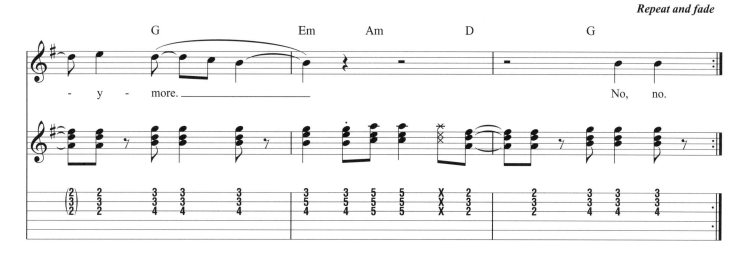

Additional Lyrics

2. When you're on a golden sea,
   You don't need no memory,
   Just a place to call your own
   As we drift into the zone.

Helter Skelter

Words and Music by John Lennon and Paul McCartney

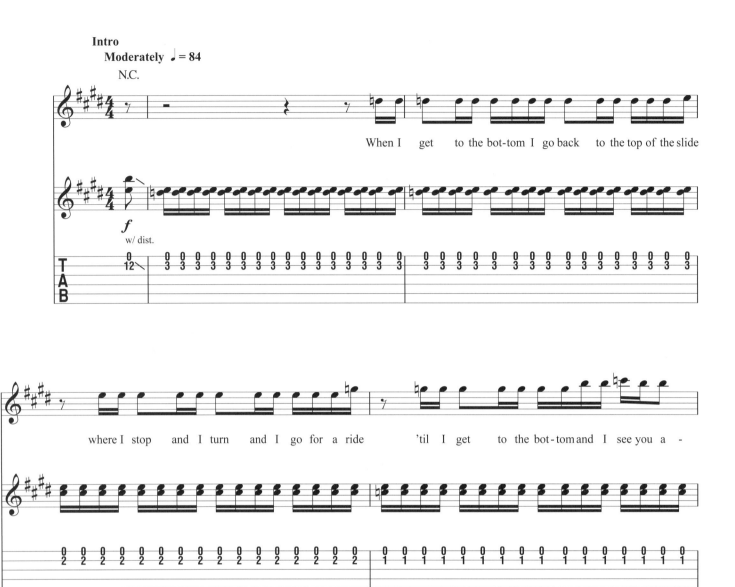

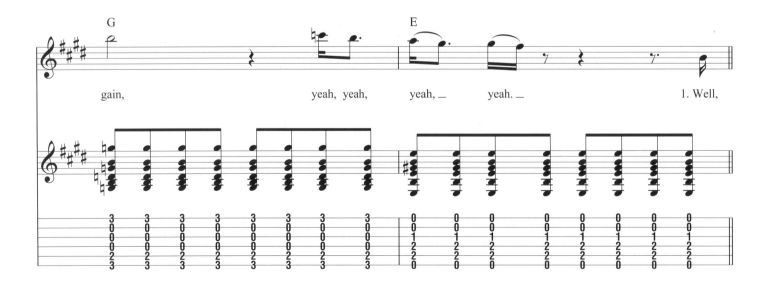

Copyright © 1968 Sony/ATV Music Publishing LLC
Copyright Renewed
All Rights Administered by Sony/ATV Music Publishing LLC, 424 Church Street, Suite 1200, Nashville, TN 37219
International Copyright Secured   All Rights Reserved

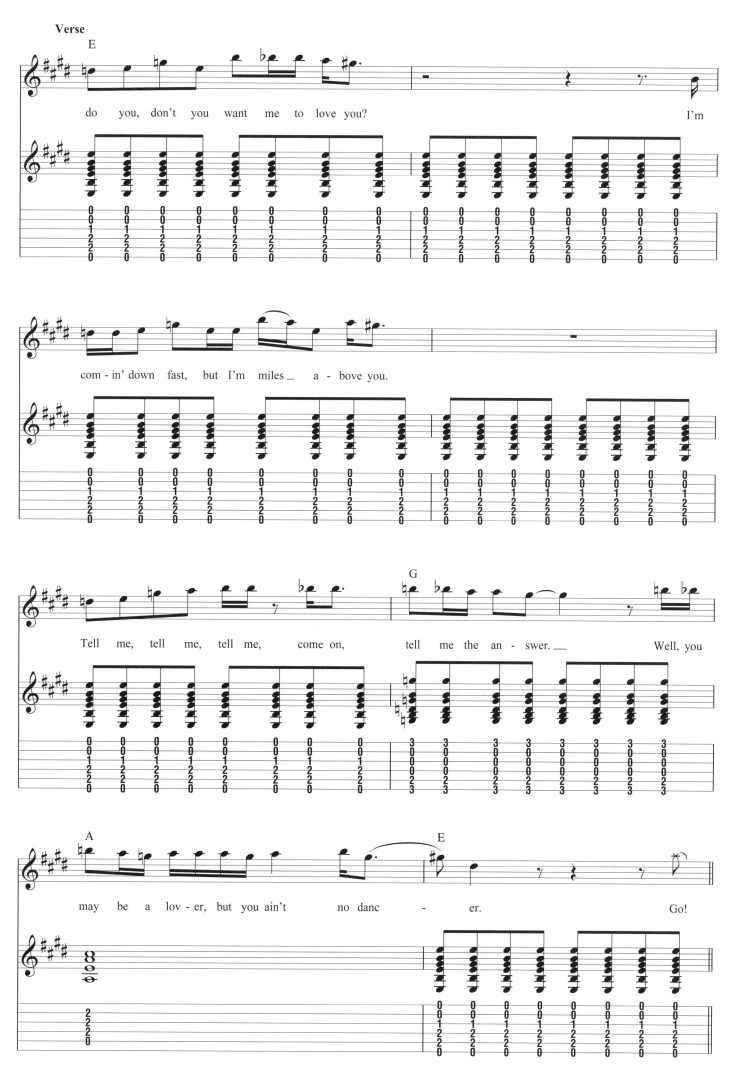

Chorus

Hel - ter skel - ter. Hel - ter skel - ter.

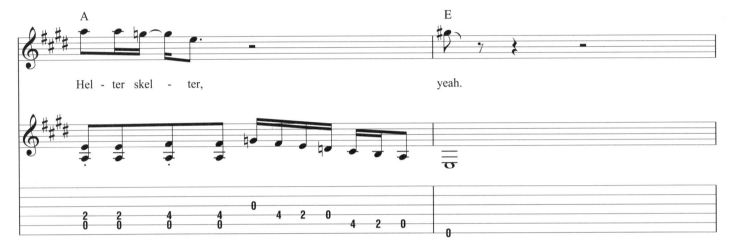

Hel - ter skel - ter, yeah.

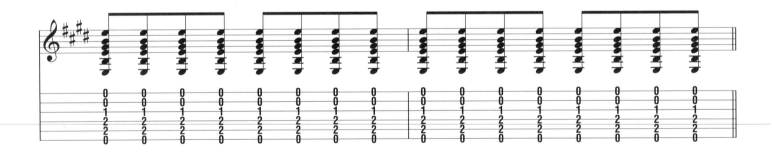

Verse

2. Will you, won't you want me to make you?
3. *See additional lyrics*

I'm

com - in' down fast but don't let me break you.

Tell me, tell me, tell me the an - swer. Ya may be a lov - er but you ain't no danc - er.

Chorus

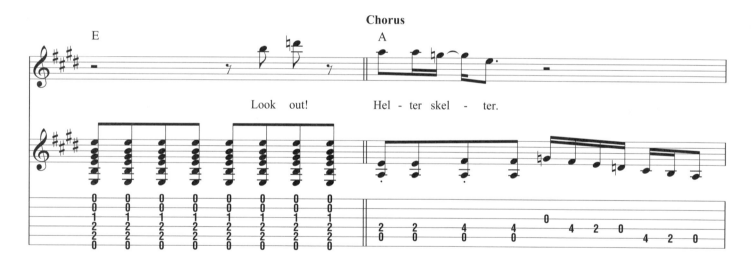

Look out! Hel - ter skel - ter.

To Coda ⊕

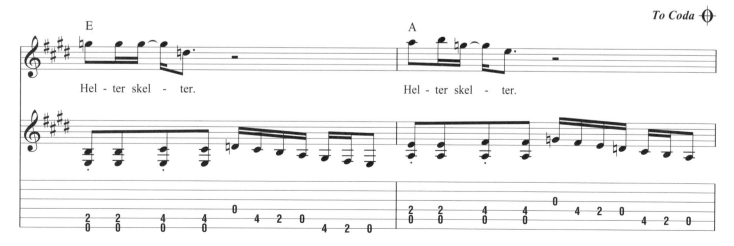

Hel - ter skel - ter.   Hel - ter skel - ter.

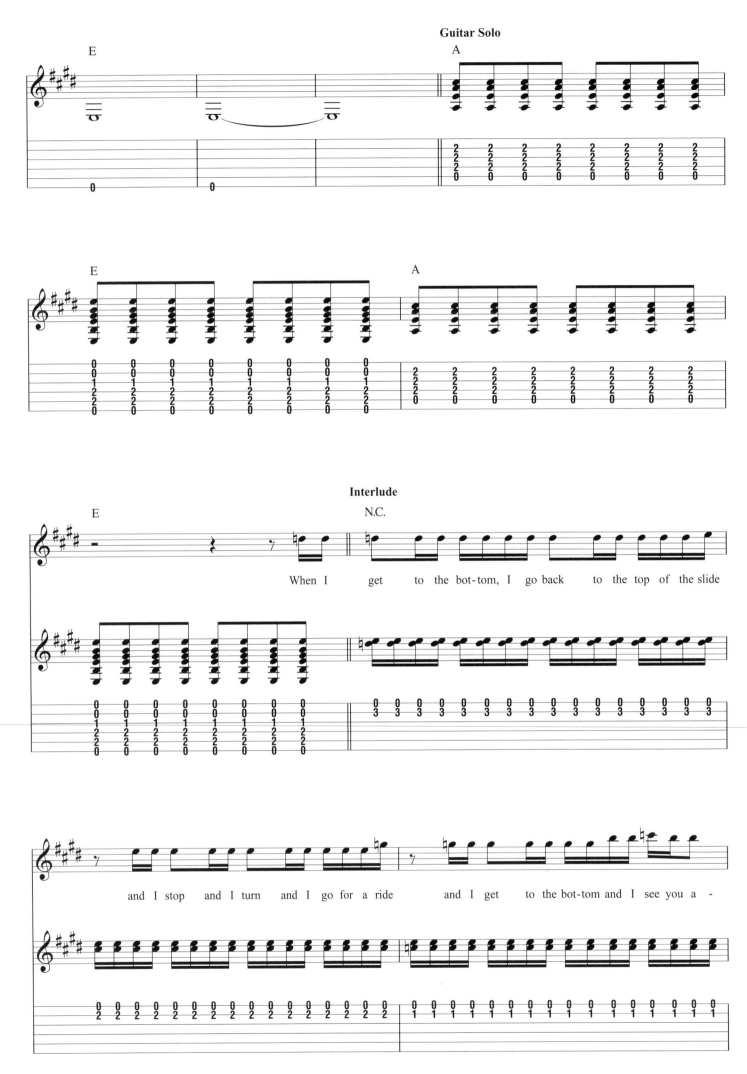

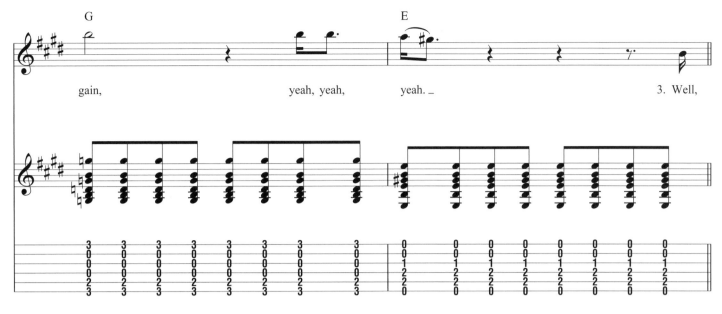

 Coda

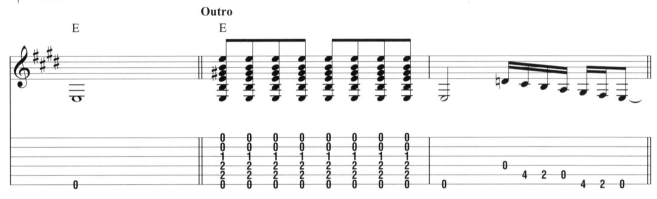

Repeat and fade

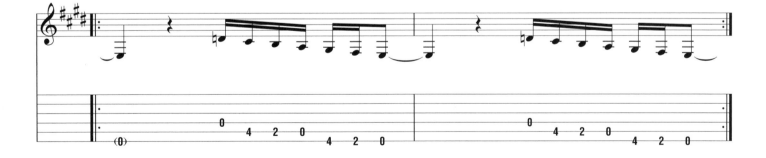

Additional Lyrics

3. Well, do you, don't you want me to make you?
   I'm comin' down fast, but don't let me break you.
   Tell me, tell me, tell me the answer.
   Ya may be a lover but you ain't no dancer. Look out!

Hey Joe

Words and Music by Billy Roberts

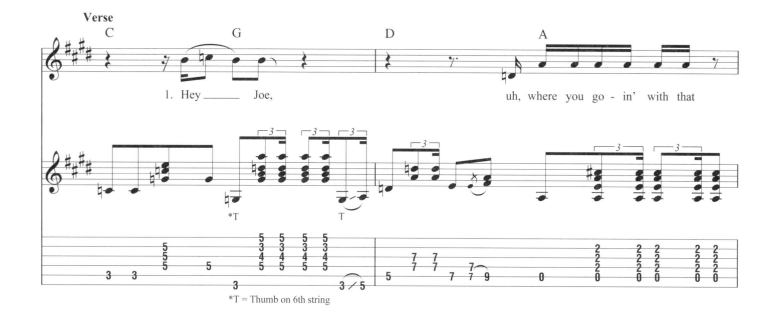

*T = Thumb on 6th string

Copyright © 1962 Third Palm Music and Ensign Music
Copyright Renewed
All Rights Administered by BMG Rights Management (US) LLC
All Rights Reserved   Used by Permission

I said where you go - in' with that gun in your hand? _ Al - right.

I'm go - in' down to shoot my old la - dy, _

you know I caught her mess - in' _ 'round with an - oth - er man.

Yeah!

I'm go - in' down to shoot my old la - dy,

you know I caught her mess - in' 'round with an - oth - er man. ___ Huh! And that ain't

Verse

too cool. 2. Uh, hey ___ Joe,

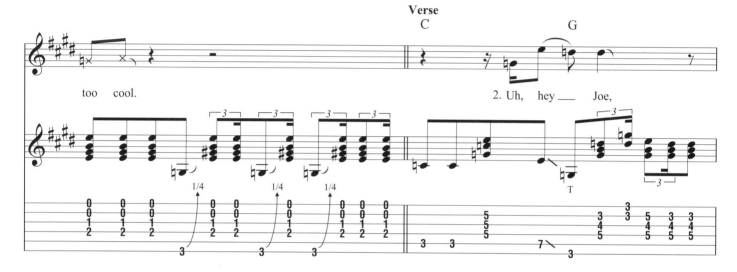

I heard you ___ shot your wom - an down, you shot her down now. ___

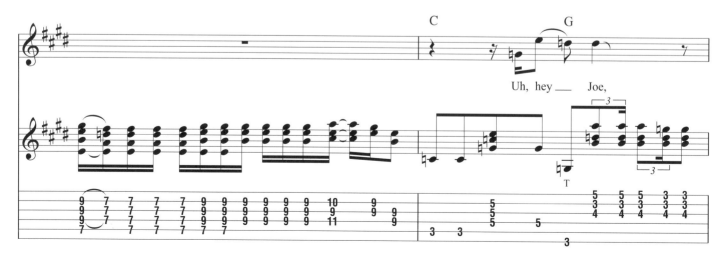

Uh, hey ___ Joe,

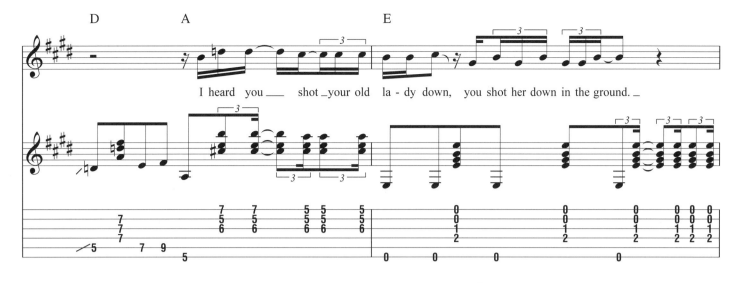

I heard you __ shot __ your old la - dy down, you shot her down in the ground. __

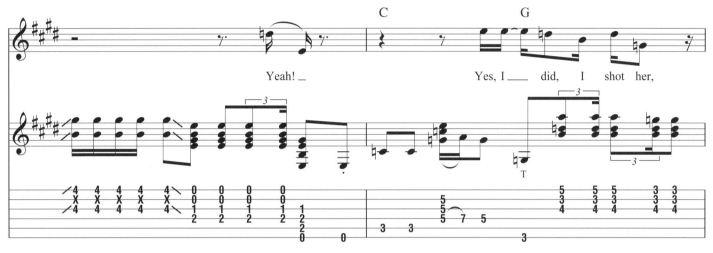

Yeah! __ Yes, I ___ did, I shot her,

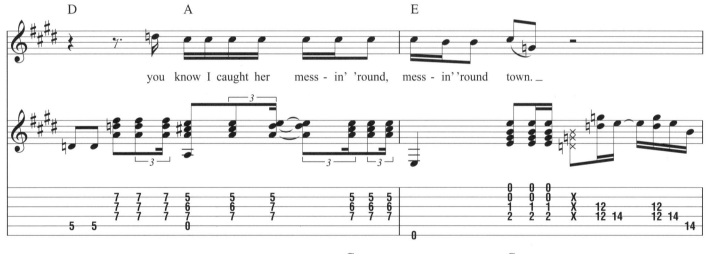

you know I caught her mess - in' 'round, mess - in' 'round town. __

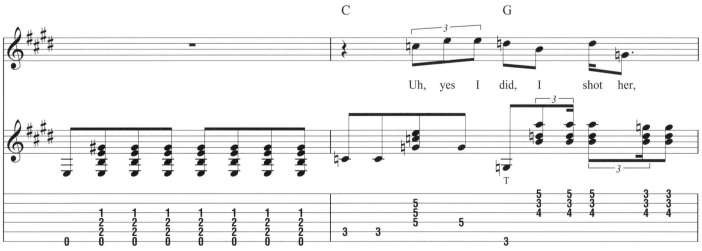

Uh, yes I did, I shot her,

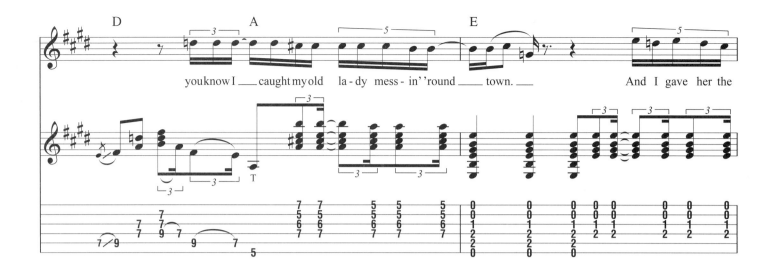

you know I ___ caught my old la - dy mess - in' 'round ___ town. ___ And I gave her the

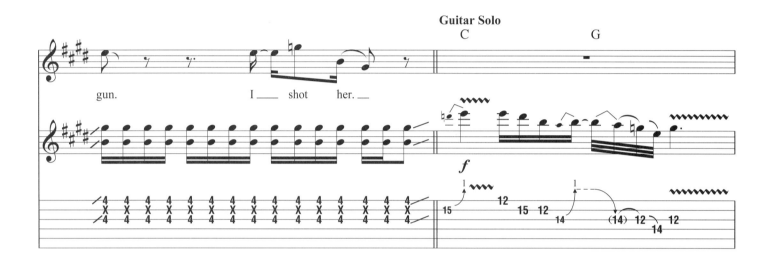

gun. I ___ shot her. ___

Guitar Solo

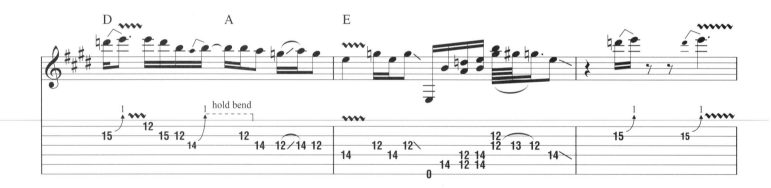

hold bend

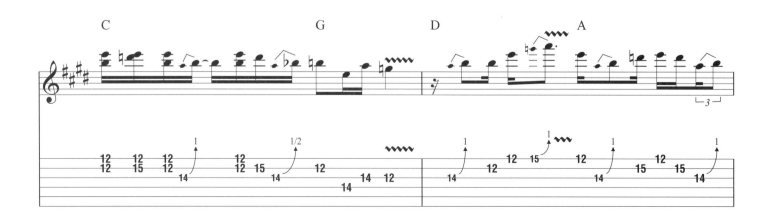

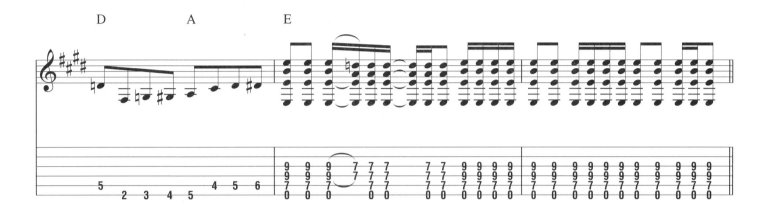

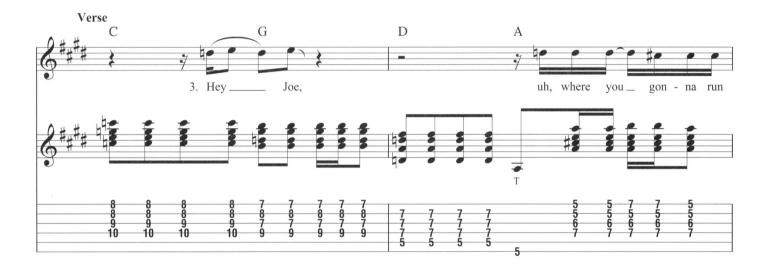

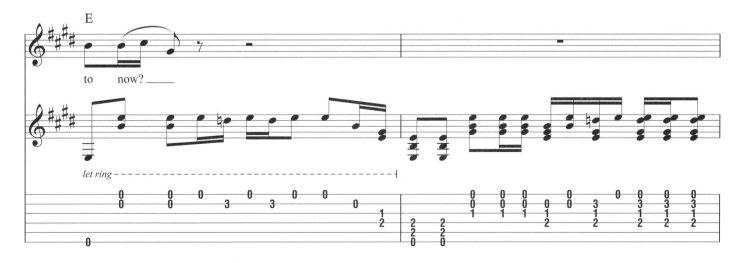

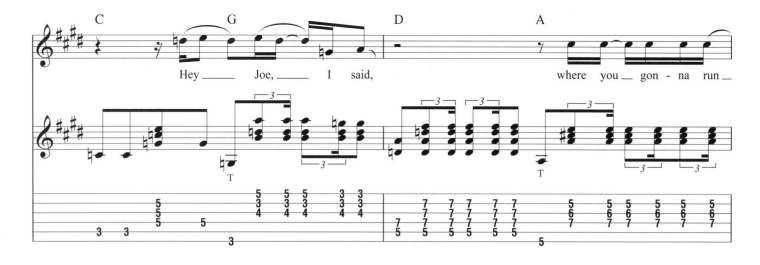

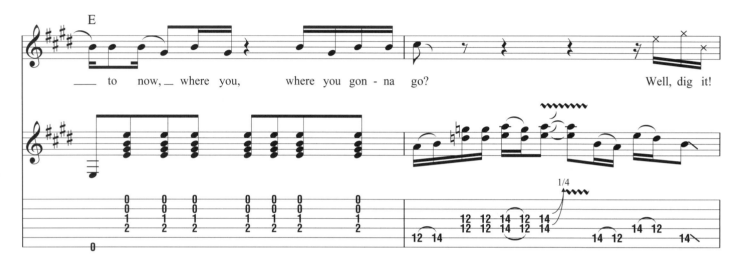

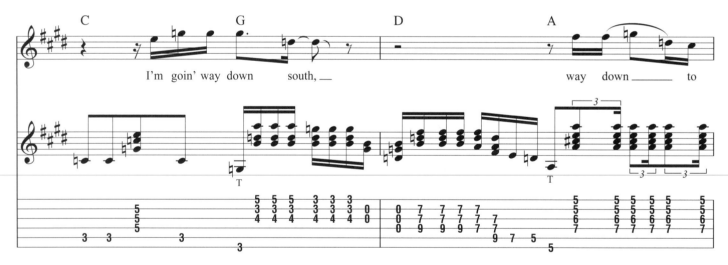

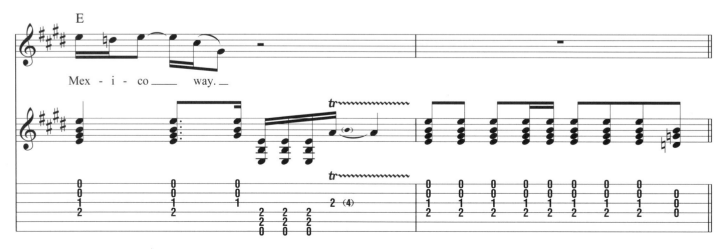

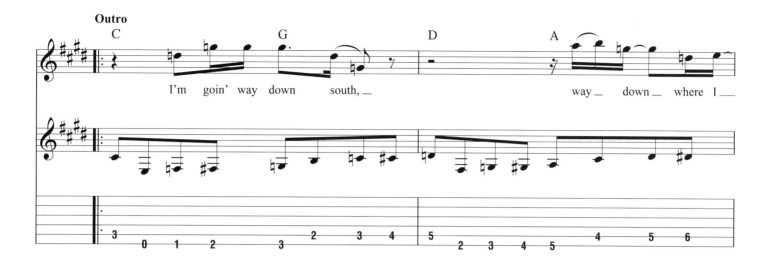

I'm goin' way down south, __ way __ down __ where I __

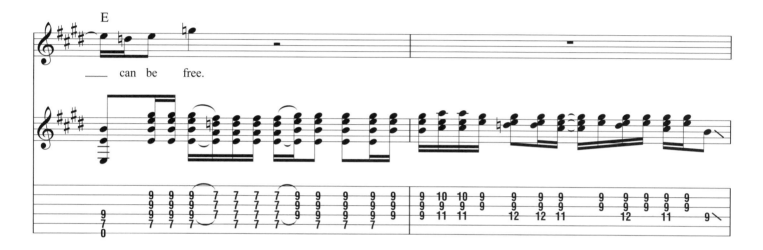

__ can be free.

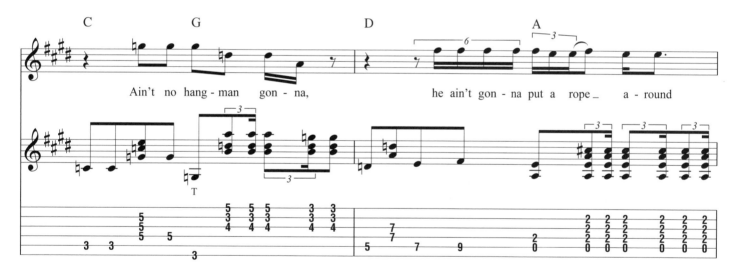

Ain't no hang - man gon - na, he ain't gon - na put a rope __ a - round

Repeat and fade

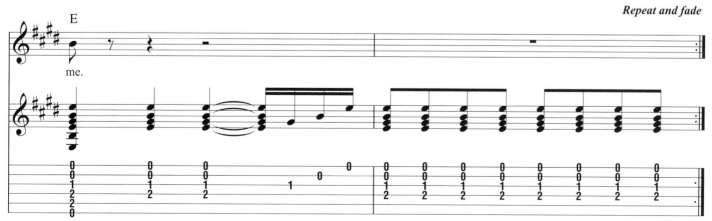

me.

Highway to Hell

Words and Music by Angus Young, Malcolm Young and Bon Scott

Copyright © 1979 by J. Albert & Son Pty., Ltd.
International Copyright Secured   All Rights Reserved

Chorus

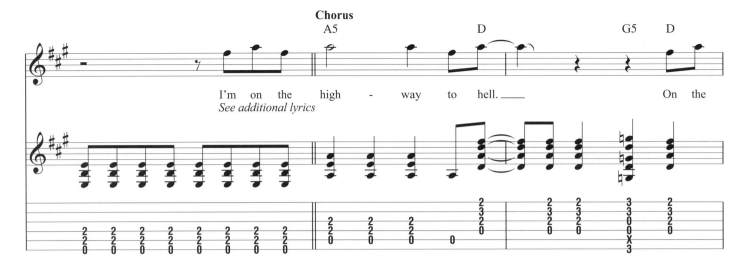

I'm on the high - way to hell. ____ On the
See additional lyrics

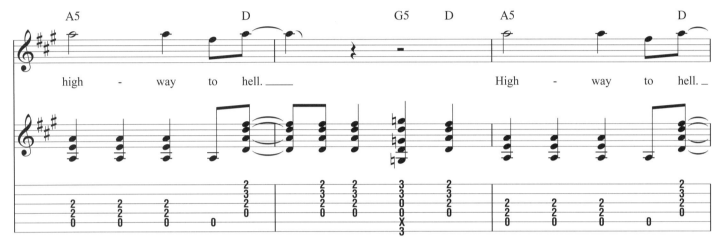

high - way to hell. ____ High - way to hell. __

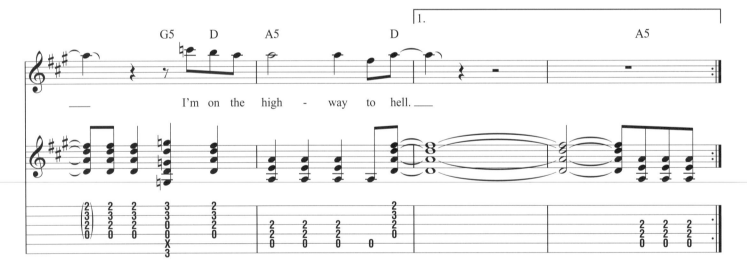

I'm on the high - way to hell. ____

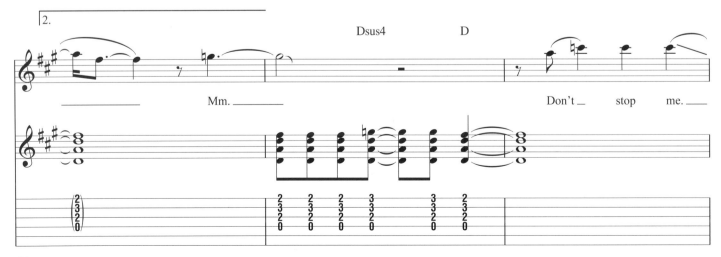

_____ Mm. _____ Don't __ stop me. ____

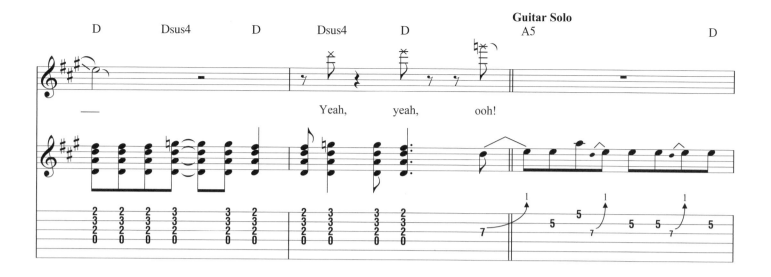

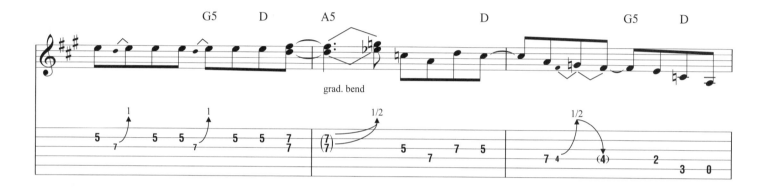

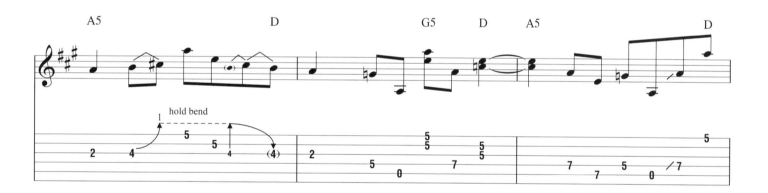

Outro-Chorus

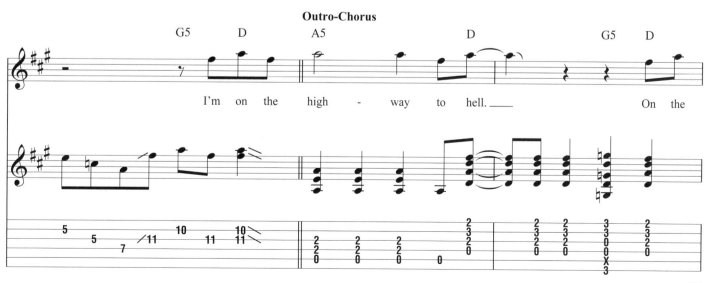

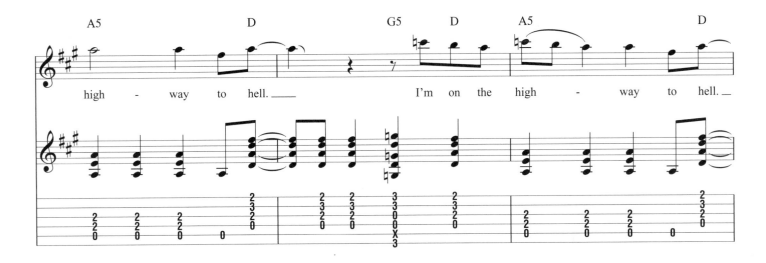

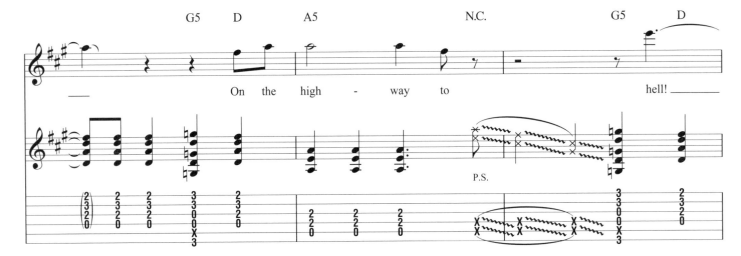

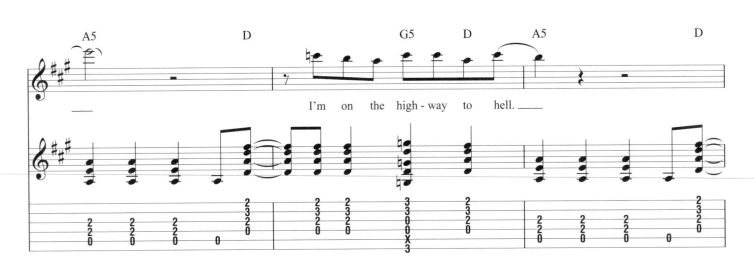

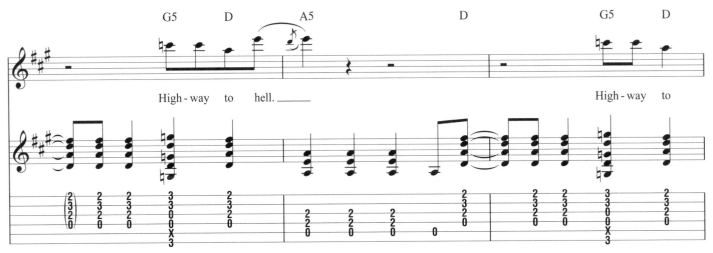

*Tremolo pick while trilling.

Additional Lyrics

2. No stop signs, speed limit, nobody's gonna slow me down.
   Like a wheel, gonna spin it, nobody's gonna mess me around.
   Hey Satan, pay'n' my dues, playin' in a rockin' band.
   Hey mama, look at me, I'm on my way to the promised land. Whoa!

Chorus I'm on the highway to hell. Highway to hell.
   I'm on the highway to hell. Highway to hell.
   Mm. Don't stop me. Yeah, yeah, ooh!

Knockin' on Heaven's Door

Words and Music by Bob Dylan

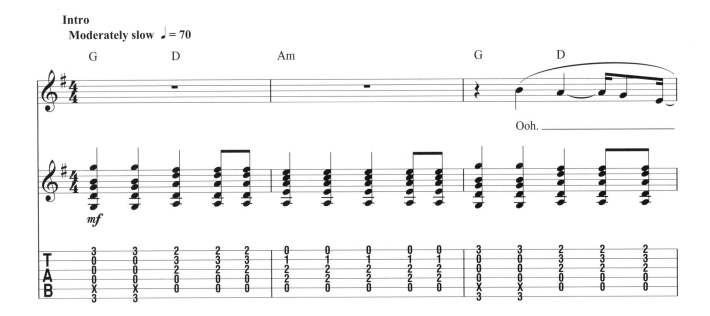

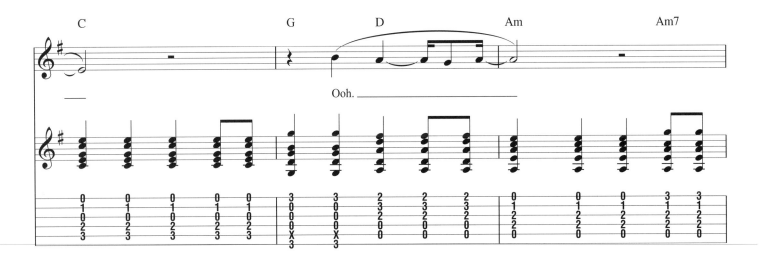

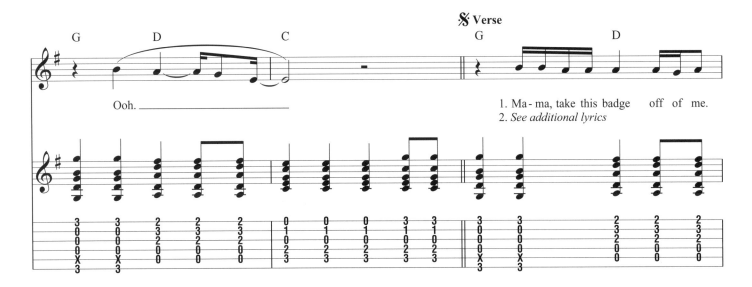

Copyright © 1973, 1976 Ram's Horn Music
International Copyright Secured   All Rights Reserved
Used by Permission

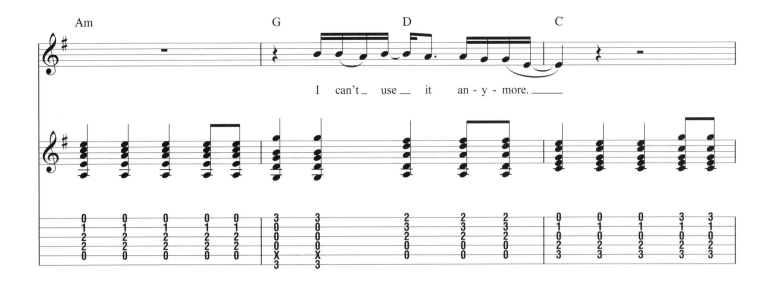

I can't_ use _ it an - y - more. ___

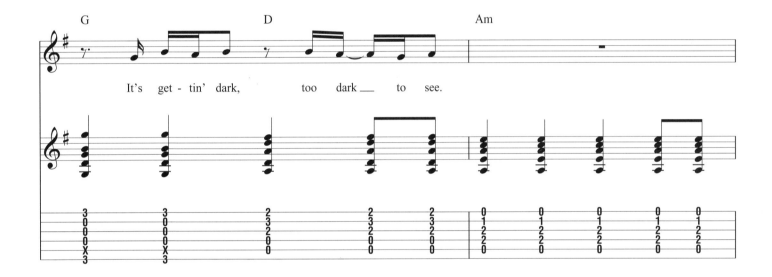

It's get - tin' dark, too dark __ to see.

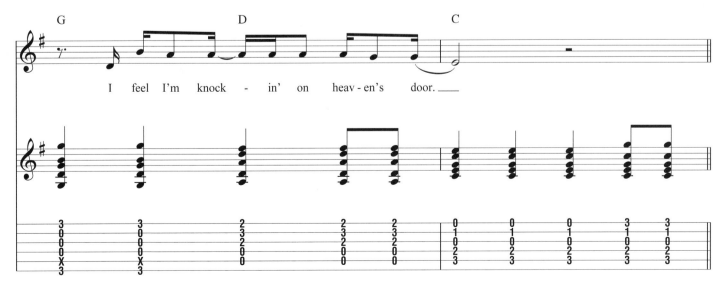

I feel I'm knock - in' on heav - en's door. ___

Chorus

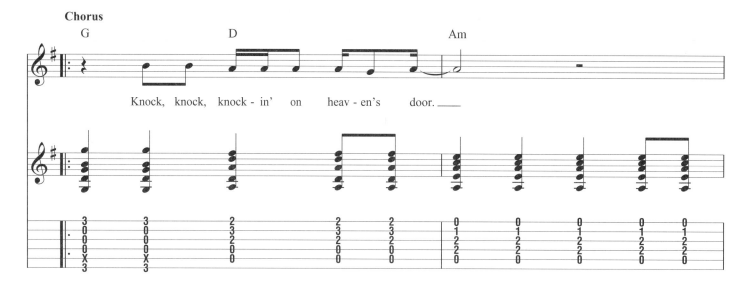

Knock, knock, knock-in' on heav-en's door. ____

2nd time, D.S.
(take repeat)

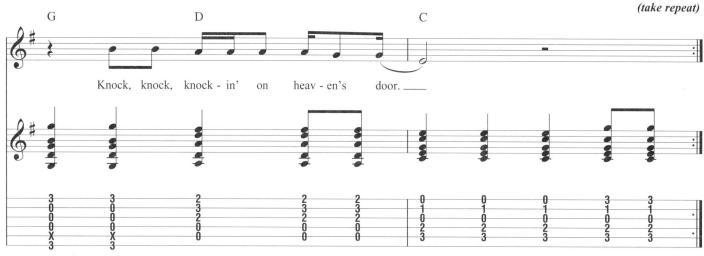

Knock, knock, knock-in' on heav-en's door. ____

Outro

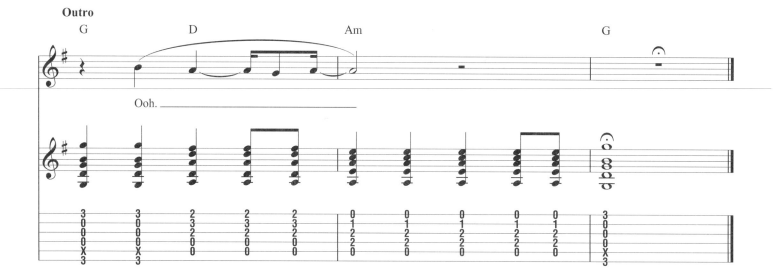

Ooh. ____

Additional Lyrics

2. Mama, put my guns in the ground.
I can't shoot them anymore.
That long black cloud is comin' down.
I feel I'm knockin' on heaven's door.

La Bamba

By Richard Valenzuela

Intro
Moderately fast Rock ♩ = 152

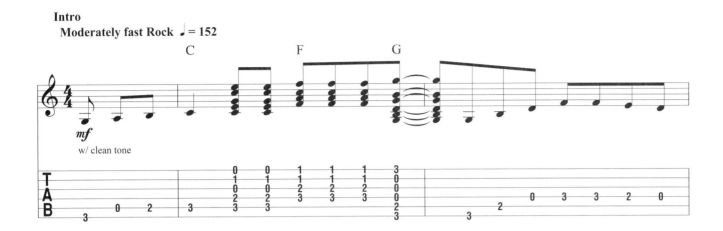

w/ clean tone

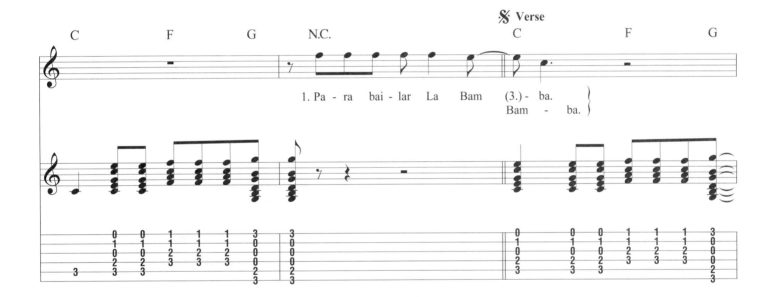

1. Pa - ra bai - lar La Bam (3.) - ba.
   Bam - ba.

Pa - ra bai - lar La Bam - ba se ne - ce - si - ta un - a po - ca — de

Copyright © 1959 EMI Longitude Music and Valens Heirs Designee
Copyright Renewed
All Rights Administered by Sony/ATV Music Publishing LLC, 424 Church Street, Suite 1200, Nashville, TN 37219
International Copyright Secured   All Rights Reserved

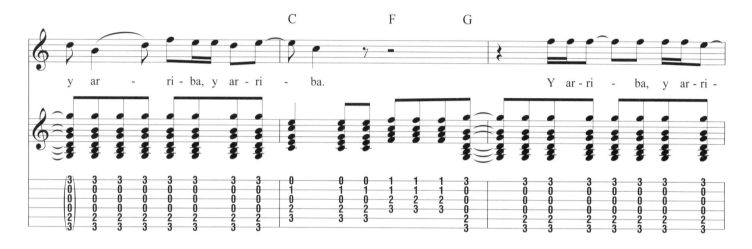

To Coda 2 ⊕

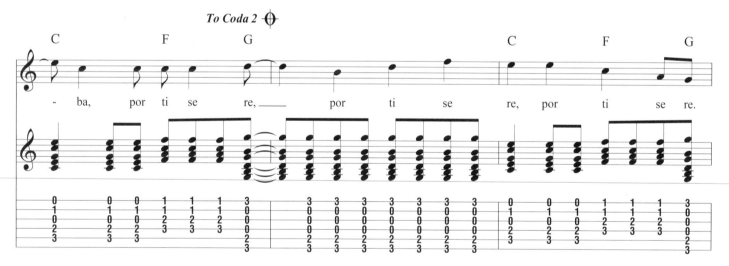

Verse

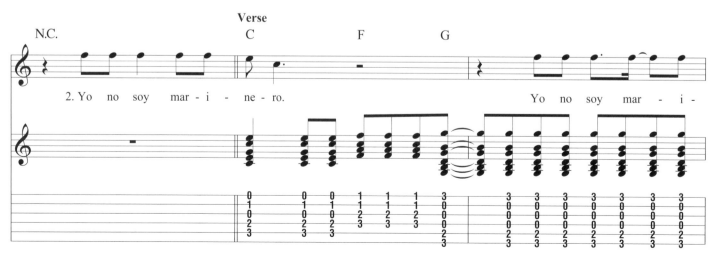

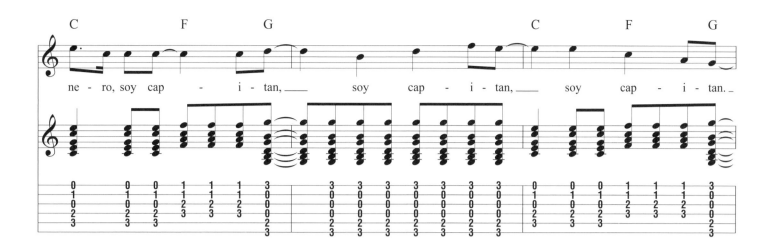

ne - ro, soy cap - i - tan,___ soy cap - i - tan,___ soy cap - i - tan.__

Chorus

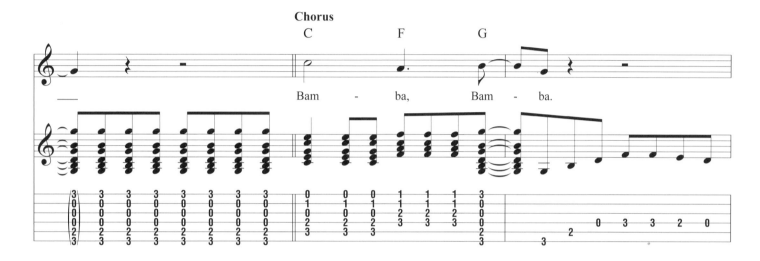

Bam - ba, Bam - ba.

Bam - ba, Bam - ba. Bam - ba, Bam -

D.S. al Coda 1

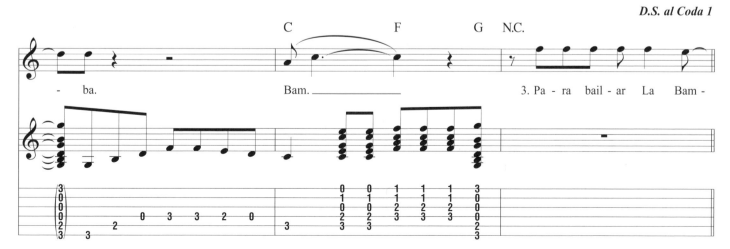

- ba. Bam.___ 3. Pa - ra bail - ar La Bam -

⊕ **Coda 1**

Guitar Solo

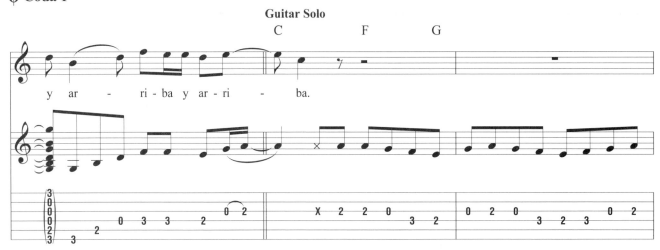

y ar - ri - ba y ar - ri - ba.

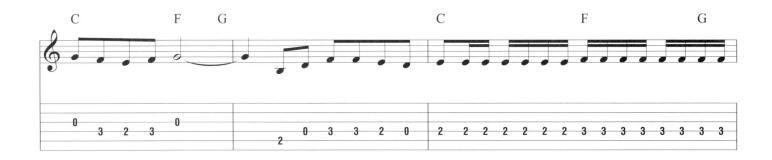

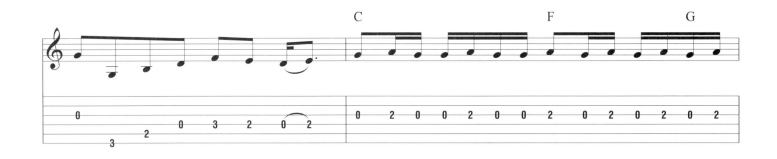

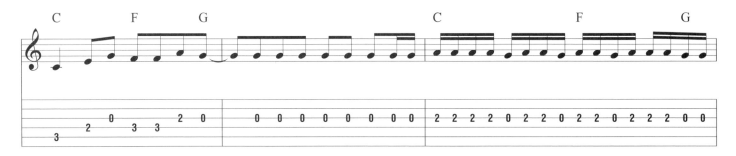

D.S. al Coda 2 **Coda 2**

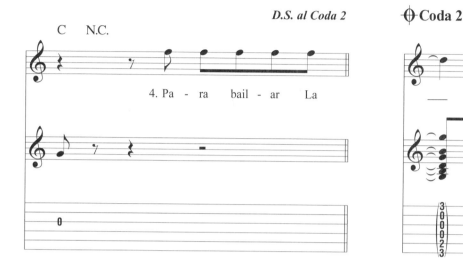

4. Pa - ra bail - ar La

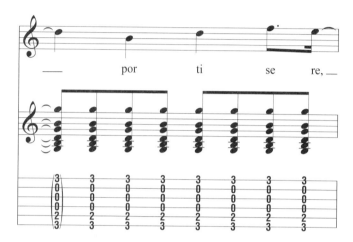

— por ti se re, —

Outro-Chorus

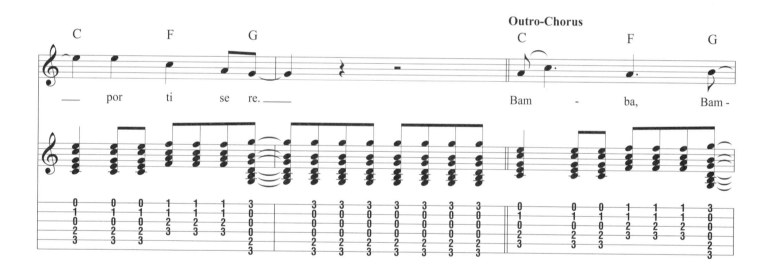

— por ti se re. —— Bam - ba, Bam -

Repeat and fade

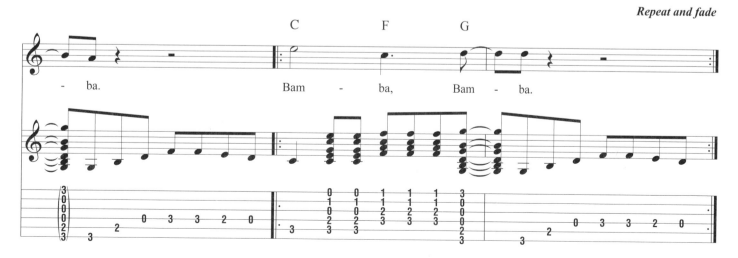

- ba. Bam - ba, Bam - ba.

Living After Midnight

Words and Music by Glenn Raymond Tipton, Robert Halford and Kenneth Downing

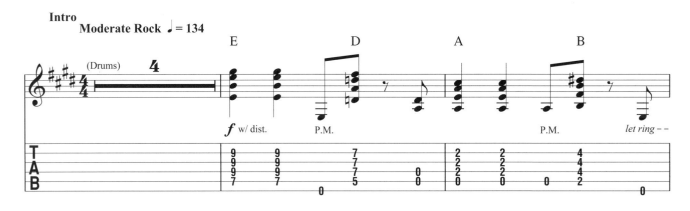

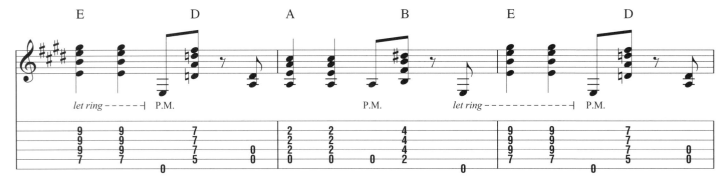

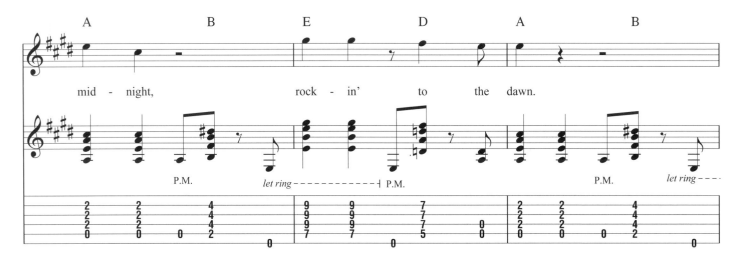

Copyright © 1980 EMI April Music Inc., Crewglen Ltd., Ebonytree Ltd. and Geargate Ltd.
All Rights Administered by Sony/ATV Music Publishing LLC, 424 Church Street, Suite 1200, Nashville, TN 37219
International Copyright Secured All Rights Reserved

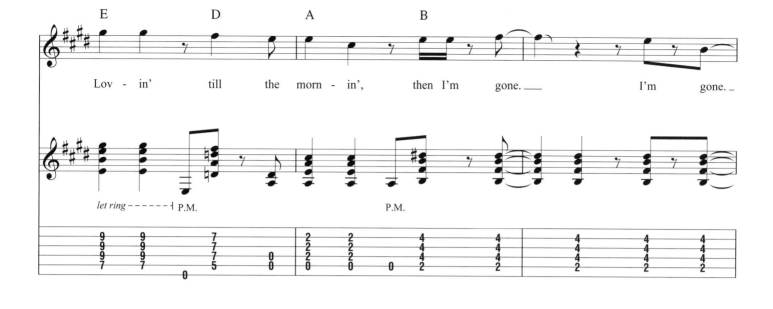

Lov - in' till the morn - in', then I'm gone. ___ I'm gone. ___

let ring - - - - - - P.M.   P.M.

⟪Verse⟫

E5

1. I took the cit - y 'bout a one A. M. ___ Load-
2., 3. *See additional lyrics*

P.M. P.M. P.M. P.M. P.M. P.M. P.M.

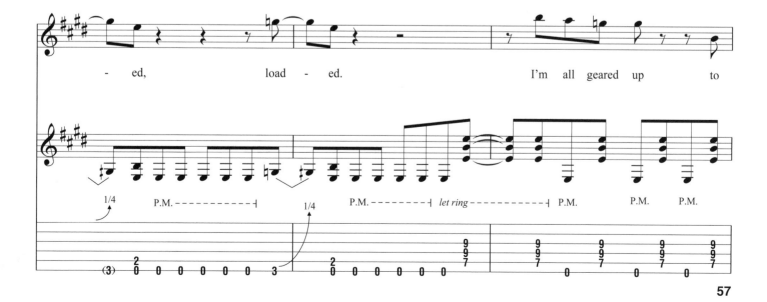

- ed,   load - ed.   I'm all geared up   to

1/4   P.M. - - - - - - - - -| 1/4   P.M. - - - - - -| *let ring - - - - - - - -|*   P.M.   P.M.   P.M.

score a - gain. __ Load - ed, load - ed.

P.M. P.M. P.M. P.M.   P.M. ⌐   ┤   P.M. ⌐   ┤

Pre-Chorus   G5   F#5   B5

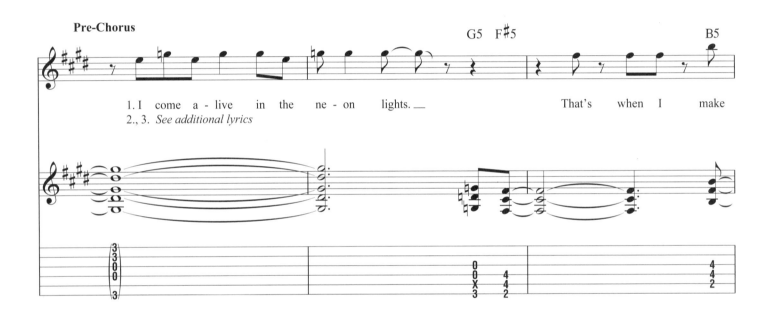

1. I come a - live in the ne - on lights. __ That's when I make
2., 3. *See additional lyrics*

Chorus

To Coda ⊕

D5   E   D   A   B

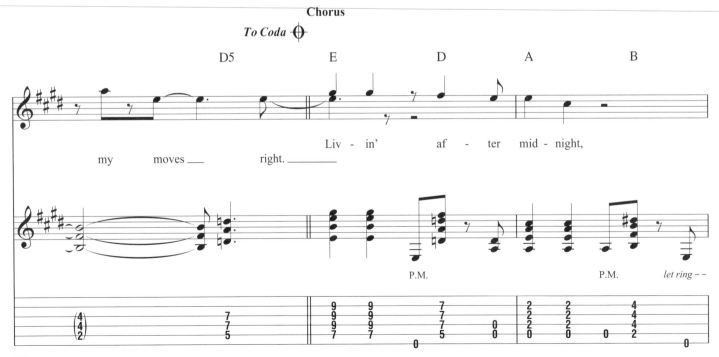

Liv - in' af - ter mid - night,

my moves __ right. _____

P.M.   P.M.   *let ring - -*

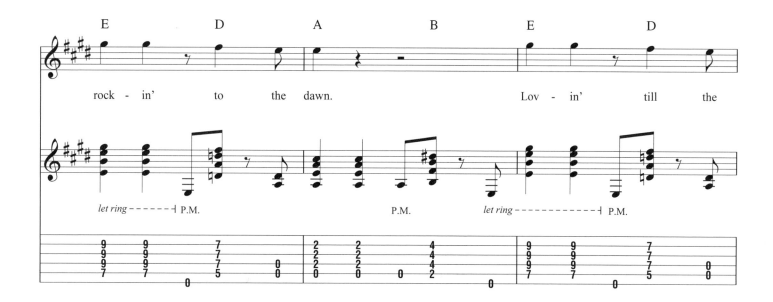

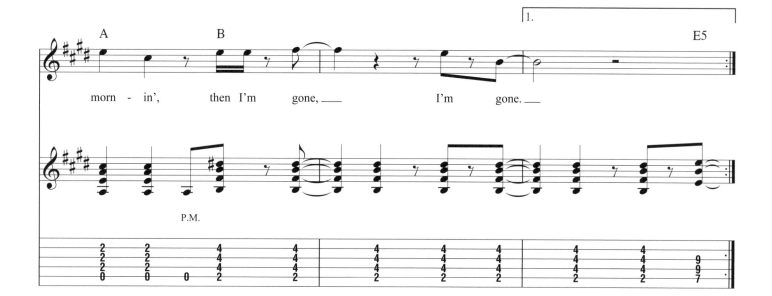

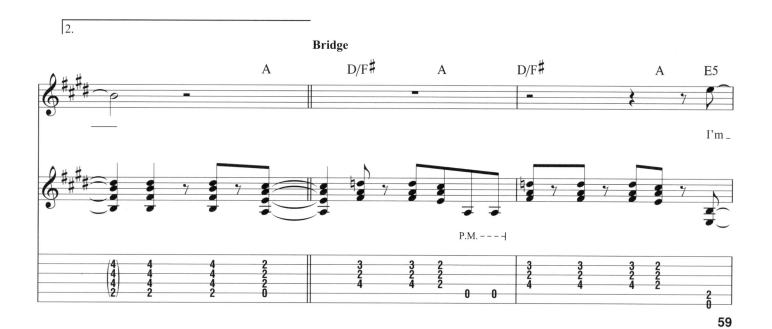

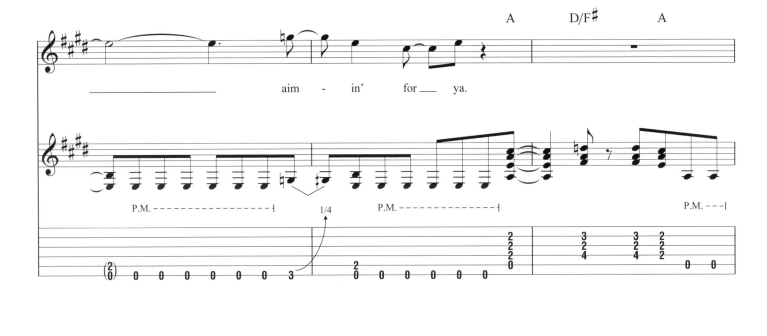

aim - in' for ___ ya.

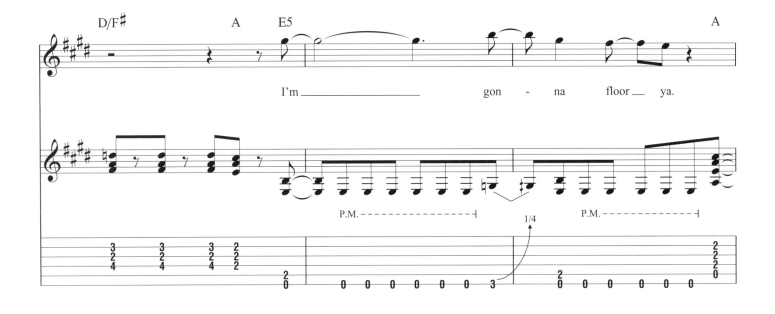

I'm ___ gon - na floor ___ ya.

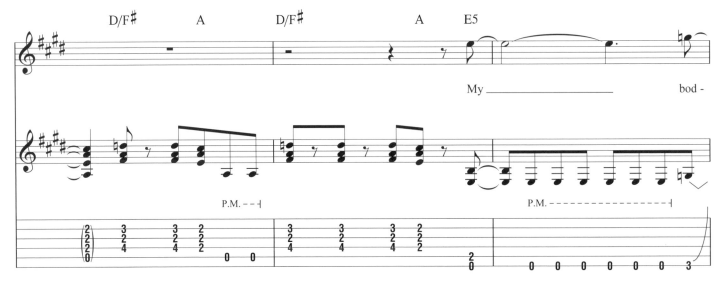

My ___ bod -

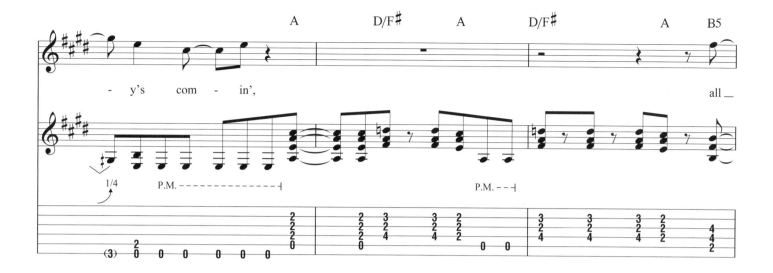

-y's com - in',   all __

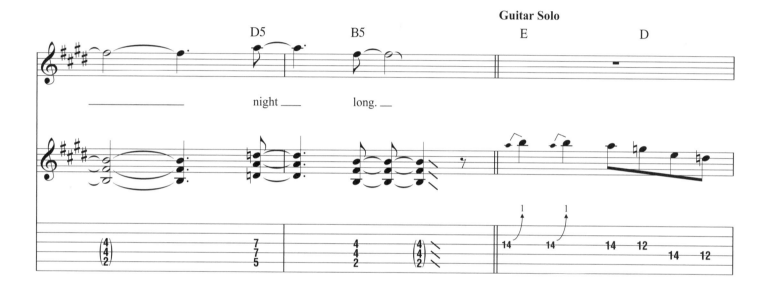

Guitar Solo

night __   long. __

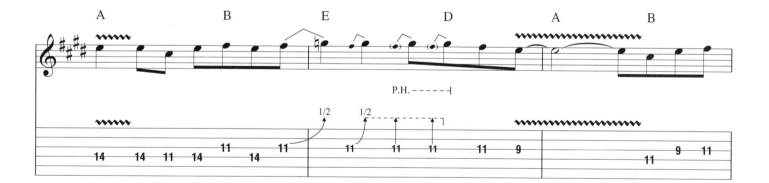

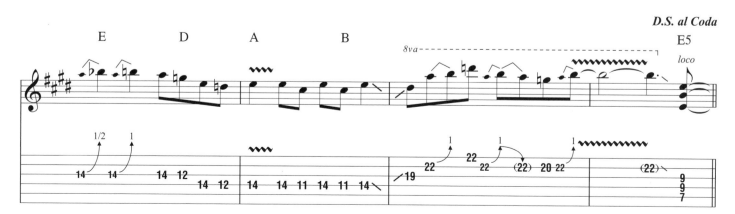

D.S. al Coda

Additional Lyrics

Additional Lyrics

2. Got gleamin' chrome reflecting feel.
   Loaded, loaded.
   Ready to take on ev'ry deal.
   Loaded, loaded.

Pre-Chorus 2. My pulse is racin', hot to take.
   But this motor's revved up, fit to break.

3. The air's electric, sparkin' power.
   Loaded, loaded.
   I'm gettin' harder by the hour.
   Loaded, loaded.

Pre-Chorus 3. I set my sights and then home in.
   The joints start fly'n' when I begin.

Should I Stay or Should I Go

Words and Music by Mick Jones and Joe Strummer

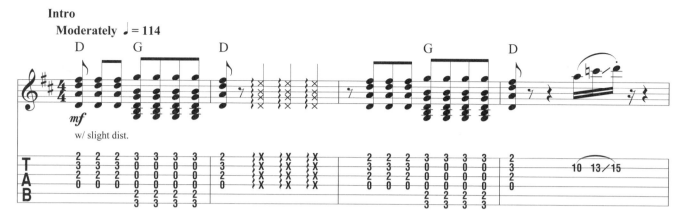

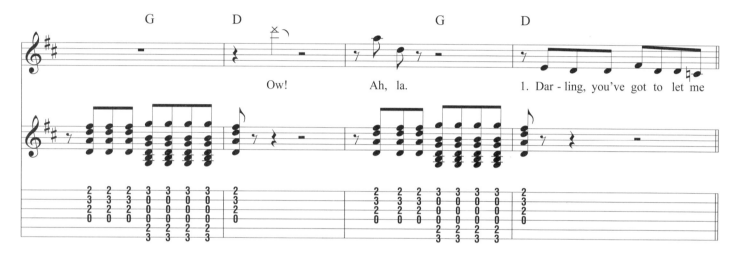

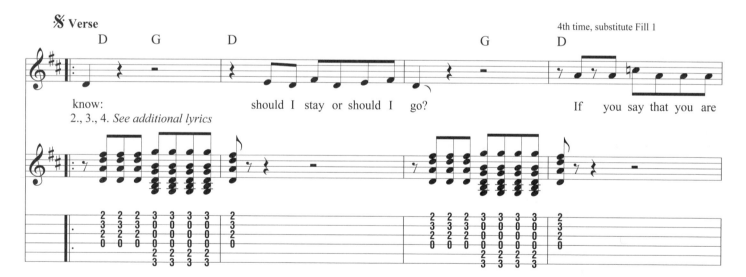

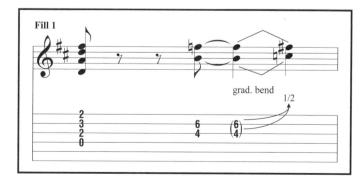

Copyright © 1982 NINEDEN LTD.
All Rights in the U.S. and Canada Controlled and Administered by UNIVERSAL - POLYGRAM INTERNATIONAL PUBLISHING, INC.
All Rights Reserved   Used by Permission

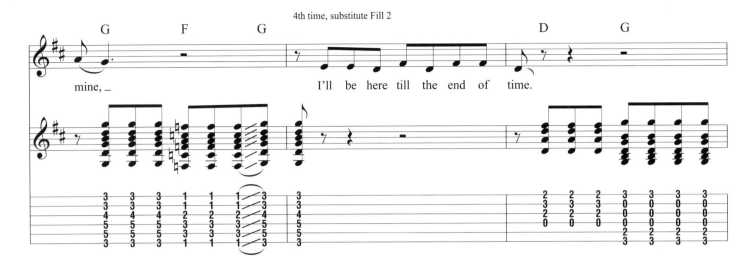

4th time, substitute Fill 2

mine, ___ I'll be here till the end of time.

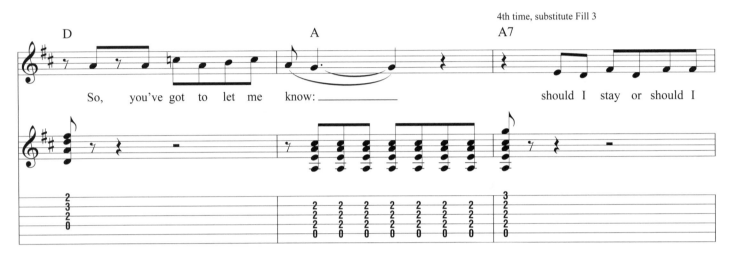

4th time, substitute Fill 3

So, you've got to let me know: _____ should I stay or should I

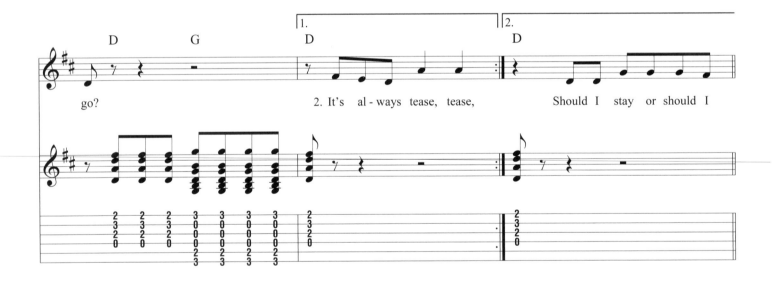

go? 2. It's al - ways tease, tease, Should I stay or should I

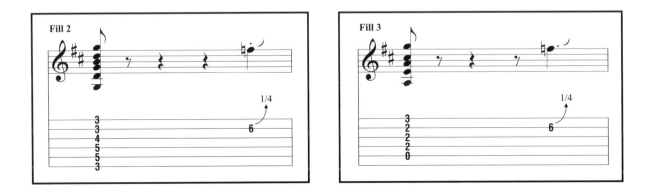

Fill 2

Fill 3

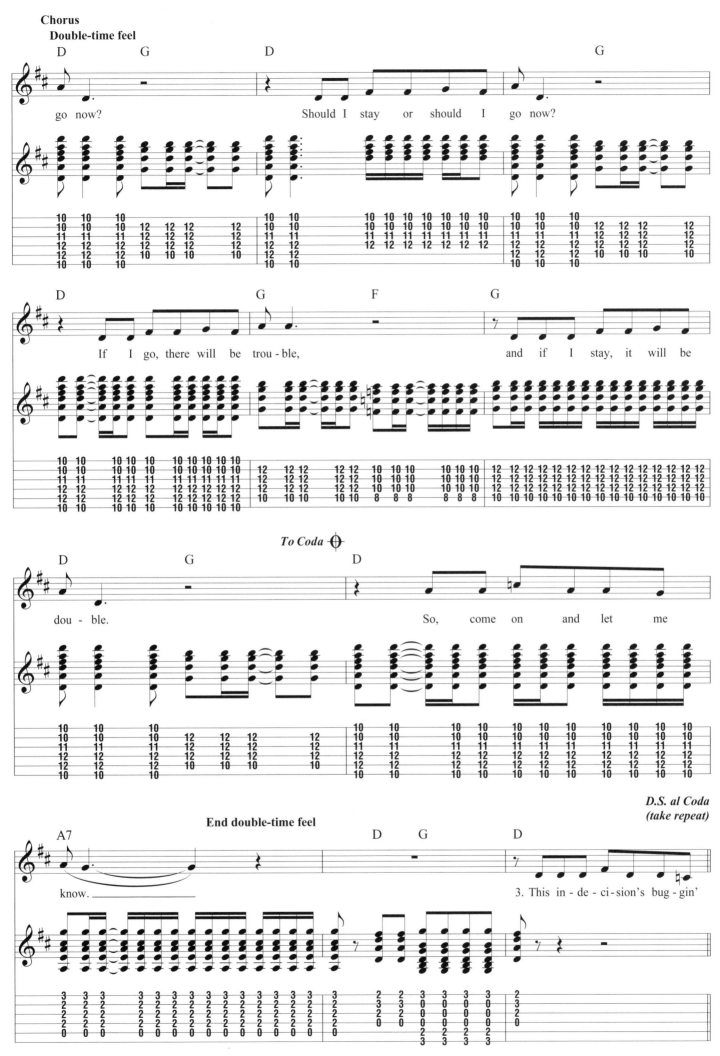

Coda

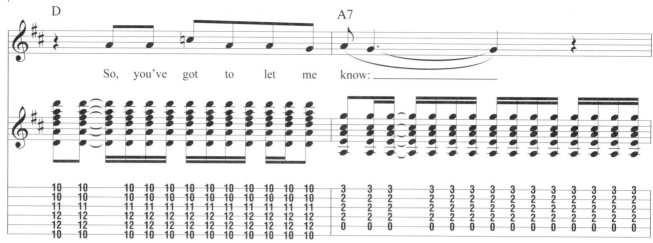

So, you've got to let me know:

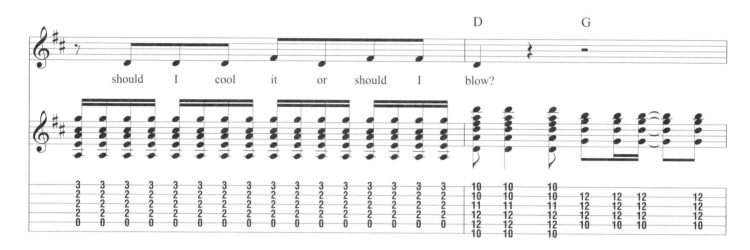

should I cool it or should I blow?

Outro-Chorus

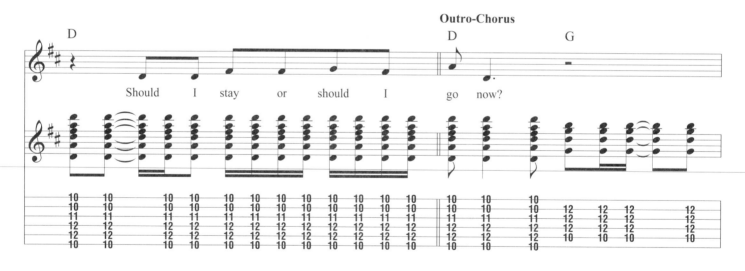

Should I stay or should I go now?

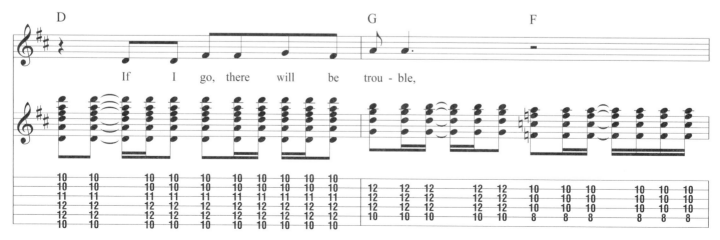

If I go, there will be trou - ble,

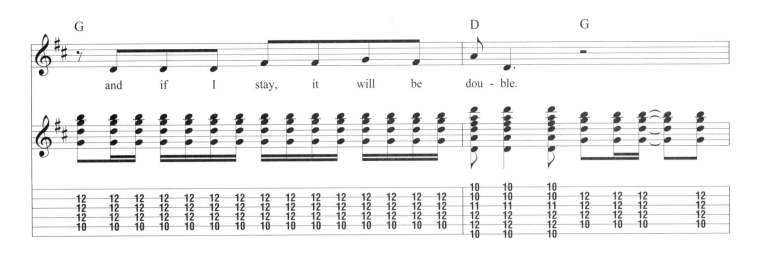

and if I stay, it will be dou - ble.

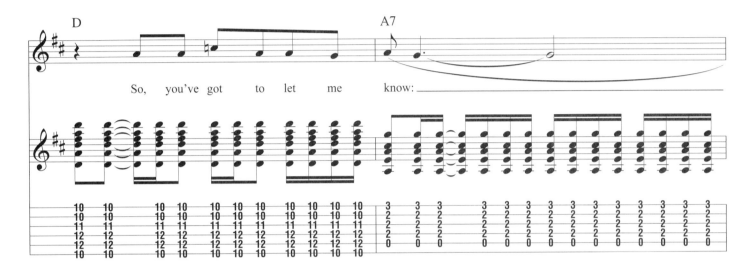

So, you've got to let me know: _____

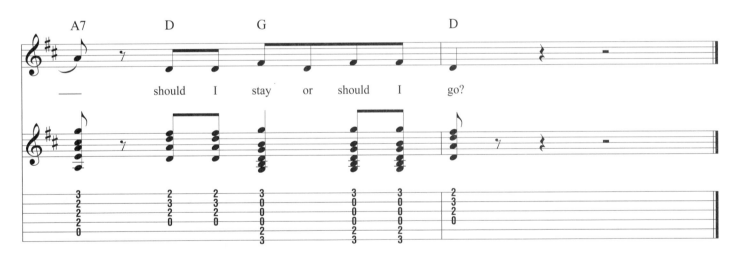

_____ should I stay or should I go?

Additional Lyrics

2. It's always tease, tease, tease.
   You're happy when I'm on my knees.
   One day is fine and next it's black.
   So if you want me off your back,
   Well, come on and let me know:
   Should I stay or should I go?

3. This indecision's buggin' me.
   If you don't want me, set me free.
   Exactly who I'm s'pose to be?
   Don't you know which clothes even fit me?
   Come on and let me know:
   Should I cool it or should I blow?

4. *Instrumental*

Oh, Pretty Woman

Words and Music by Roy Orbison and Bill Dees

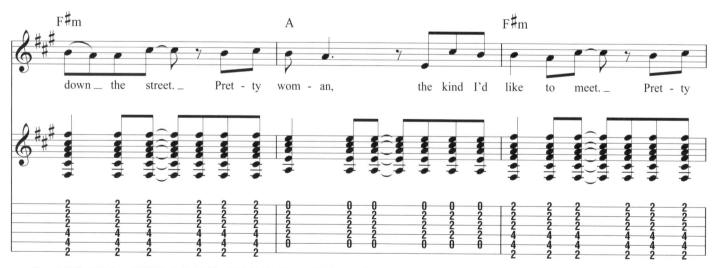

Copyright © 1964 Sony/ATV Music Publishing LLC, R Key Darkus Publishing, Orbi Lee Publishing, Barbara Orbison Music Publishing and Roys Boys LLC
Copyright Renewed
All Rights on behalf of Sony/ATV Music Publishing LLC Administered by Sony/ATV Music Publishing LLC, 424 Church Street, Suite 1200, Nashville, TN 37219
All Rights on behalf of R Key Darkus Publishing, Orbi Lee Publishing, Barbara Orbison Music Publishing and Roys Boys LLC
Administered by Songs Of Kobalt Music Publishing
International Copyright Secured All Rights Reserved

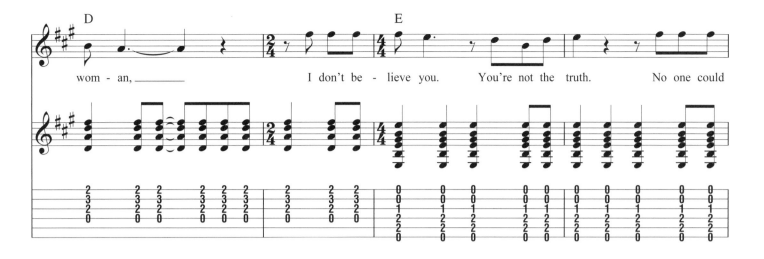

woman, _____ I don't be - lieve you. You're not the truth. No one could

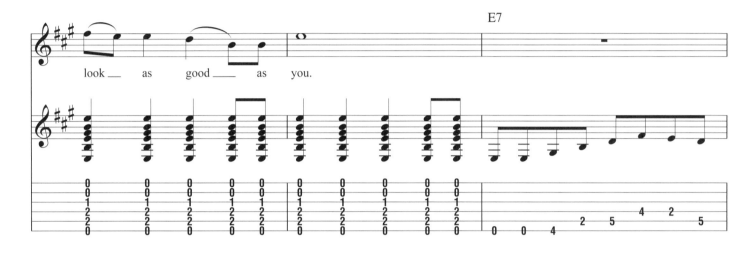

look __ as good __ as you.

Mer - cy! 2. Pret - ty

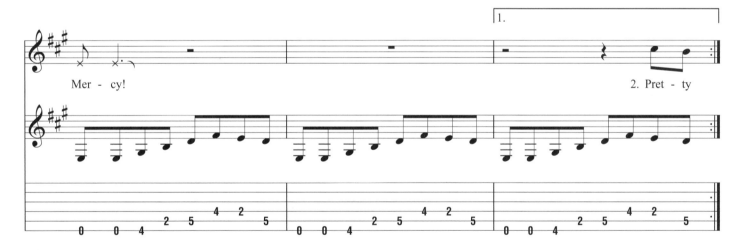

Pret - ty wom - an, stop a - while. __

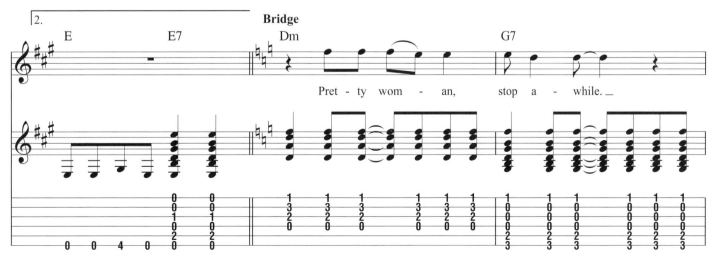

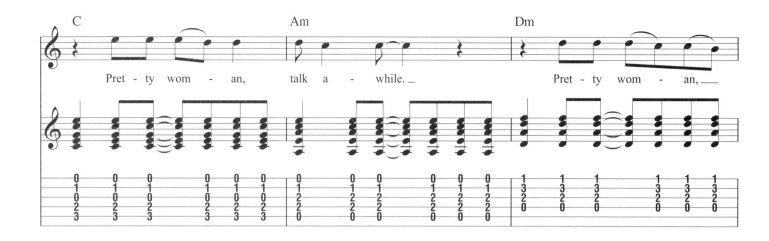

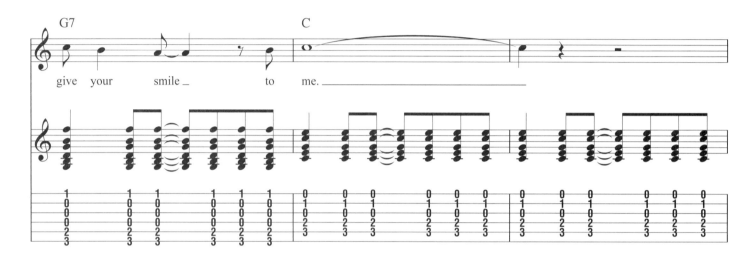

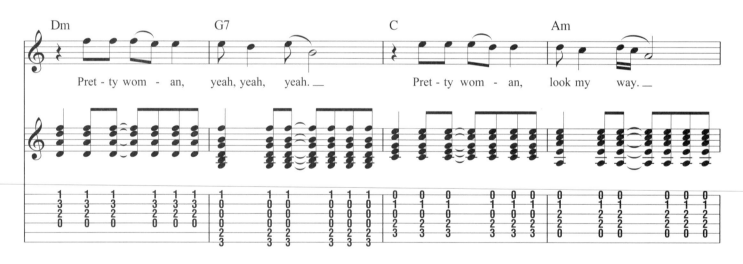

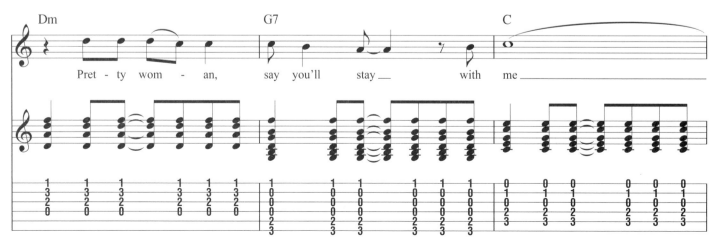

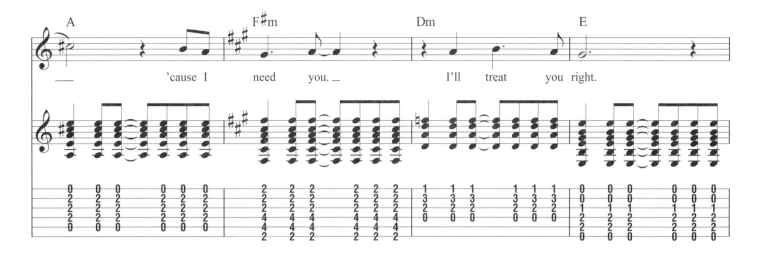

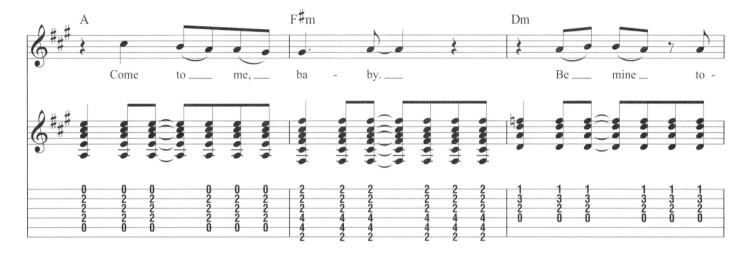

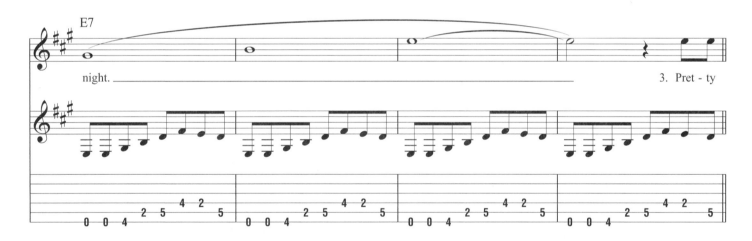

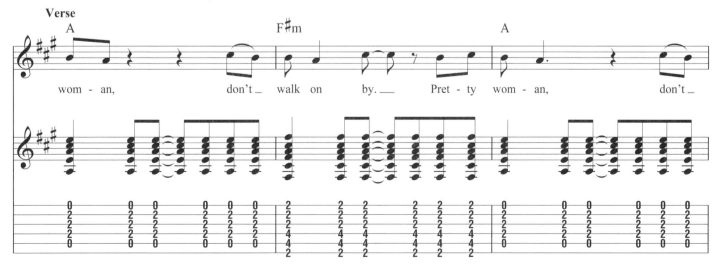

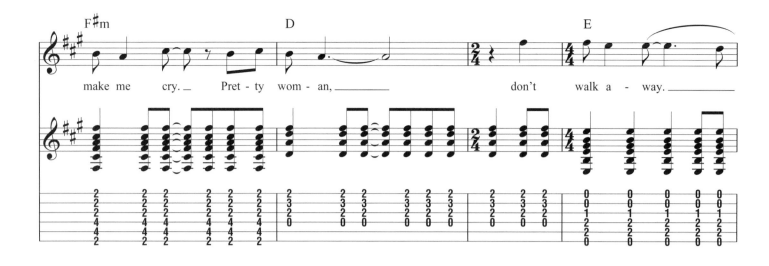

make me cry.__ Pret - ty wom - an,_____ don't walk a - way._____

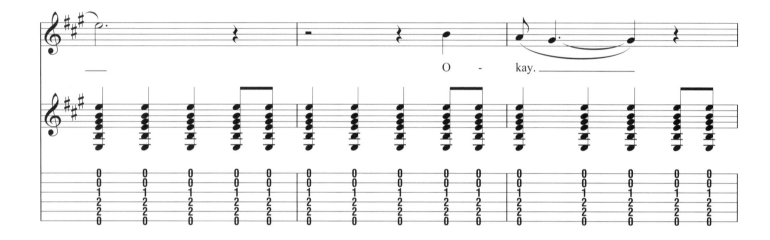

O - kay._____

If that's the way it must be, o - kay._____

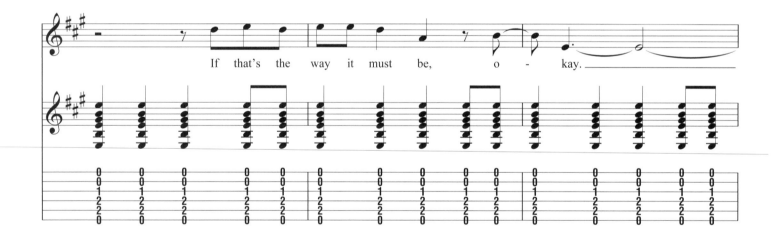

I guess I'll go __ on home, __ it's late. __ There'll be to - mor - row night,_ but

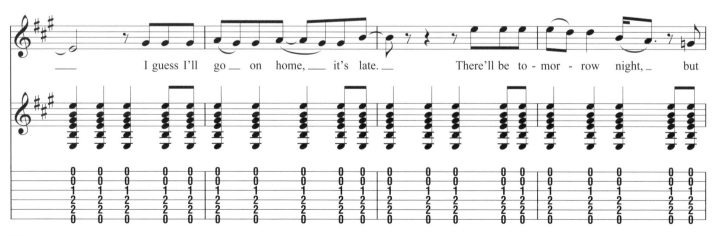

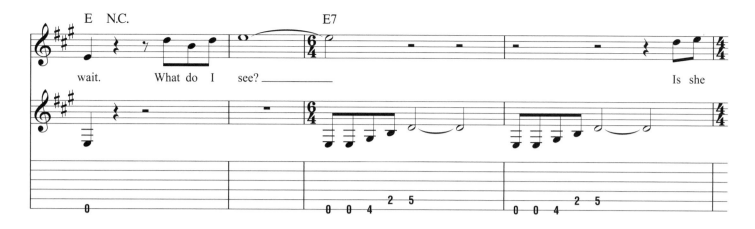

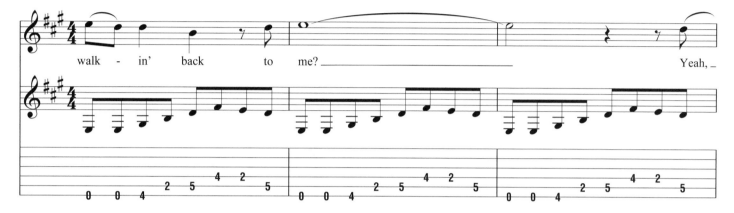

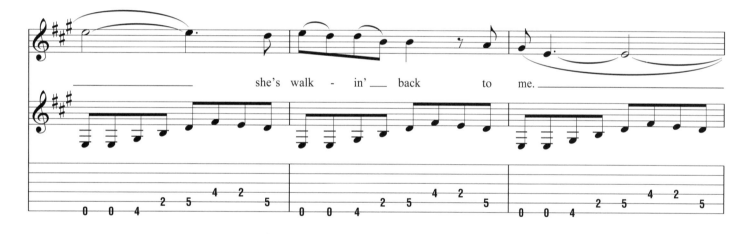

Additional Lyrics

2. Pretty woman, won't you pardon me?
   Pretty woman, I couldn't help but see;
   Pretty woman, that you look lovely as can be.
   Are you lonely just like me?

Old Time Rock & Roll

Words and Music by George Jackson and Thomas E. Jones III

Tune down 1/2 step:
(low to high) Eb-Ab-Db-Gb-Bb-Eb

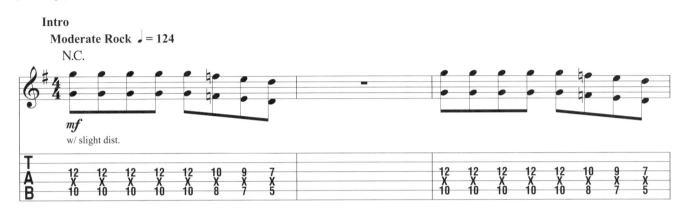

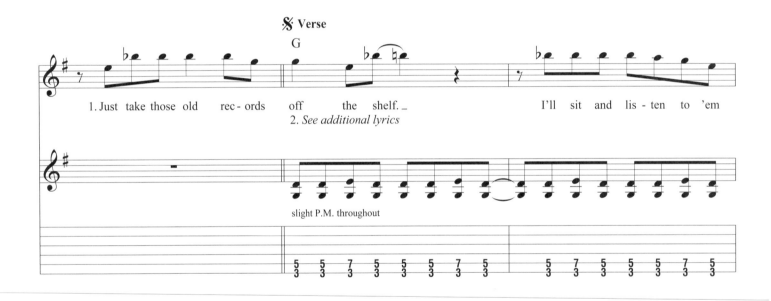

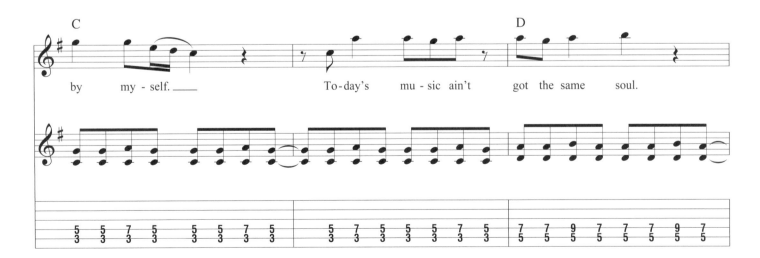

Copyright © 1977 by Peermusic III, Ltd. and Muscle Shoals Sound Publishing
Copyright Renewed
All Rights Administered by Peermusic III, Ltd.
International Copyright Secured   All Rights Reserved

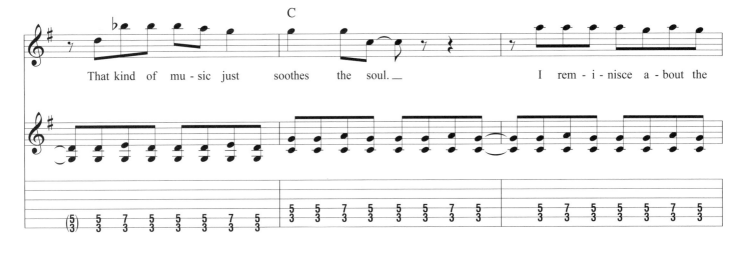

That kind of mu - sic just soothes the soul. ___ I rem - i - nisce a - bout the

To Coda 1

To Coda 2

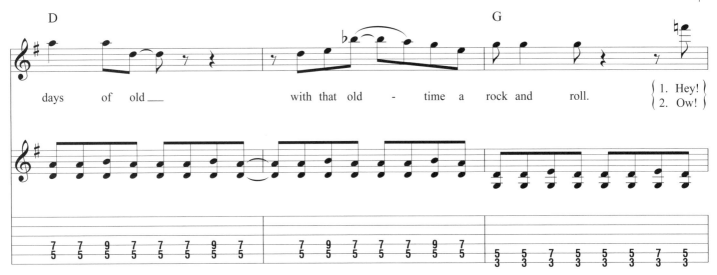

days of old ___ with that old - time a rock and roll.

{ 1. Hey! }
{ 2. Ow! }

Guitar Solo

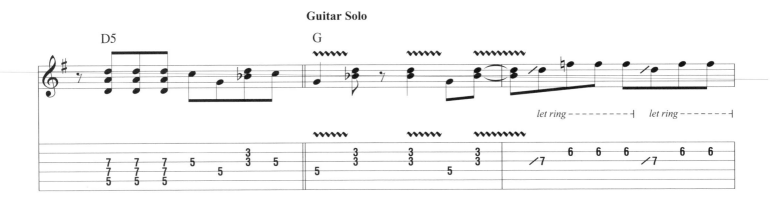

let ring - - - - - - - - -   *let ring - - - - - - -*

let ring - - - *let ring - - -*   *let ring - - - - - - - - - -*

76

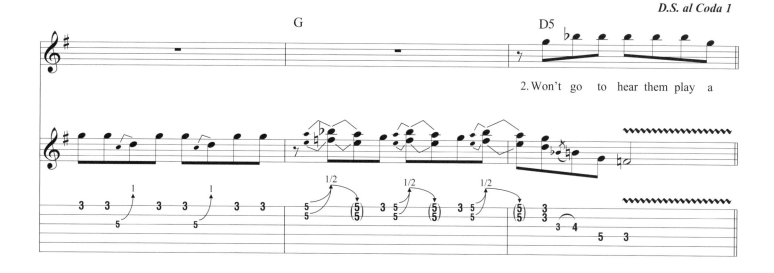

2. Won't go to hear them play a

Coda 1

Saxophone Solo

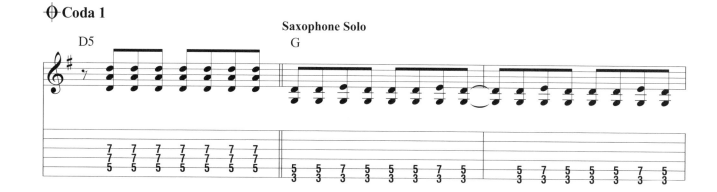

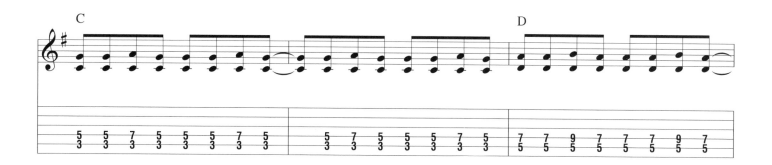

Still like that old - time a

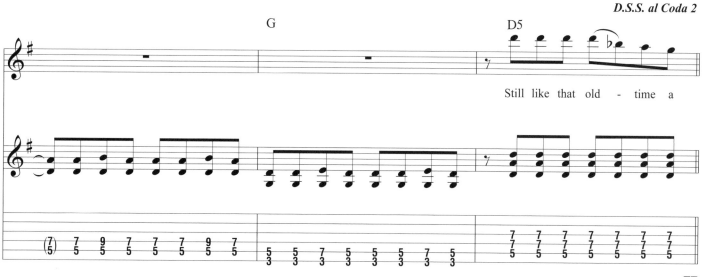

Breakdown-Chorus

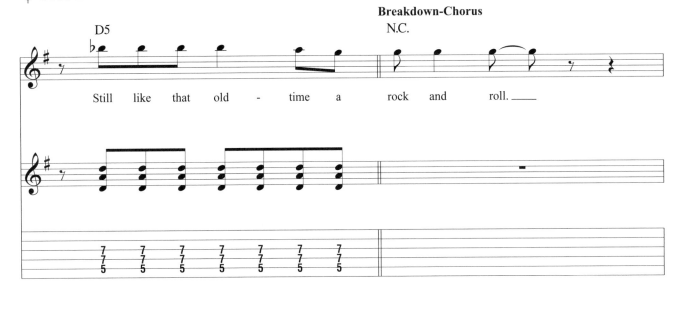

Still like that old - time a rock and roll. ____

That kind of mu - sic just soothes the soul.

I rem - i - nisce a - bout the days of old ____

with that old - time a rock and roll. Hey! Still like that old - time a

Outro-Chorus

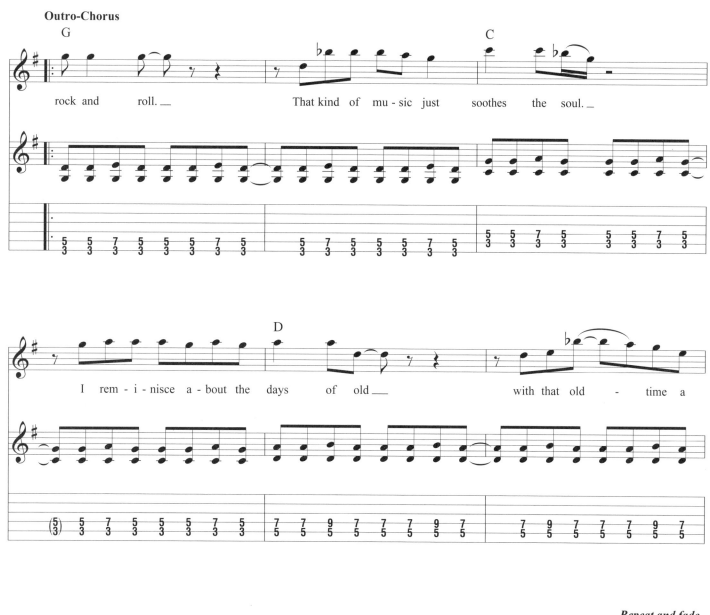

rock and roll. ___   That kind of mu - sic just soothes the soul. ___

I rem - i - nisce a - bout the days of old ___ with that old - time a

Repeat and fade

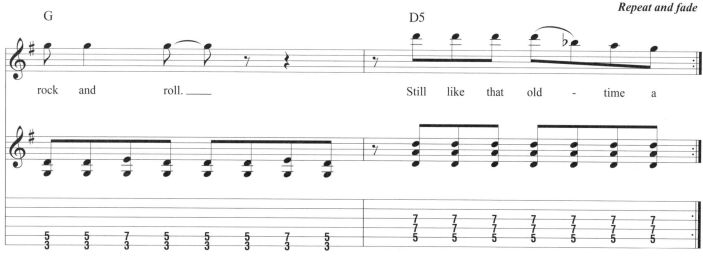

rock and roll. _____   Still like that old - time a

Additional Lyrics

2. Won't go to hear them play a tango.
   I'd rather hear some blues or funky old soul.
   There's only one sure way to get me to go:
   Start playing old time rock and roll.
   Call me a relic, call me what you will.
   Say I'm old-fashioned, say I'm over the hill.
   Today's music ain't got the same soul.
   I like that old time rock and roll.

Smells Like Teen Spirit

Words and Music by Kurt Cobain, Krist Novoselic and Dave Grohl

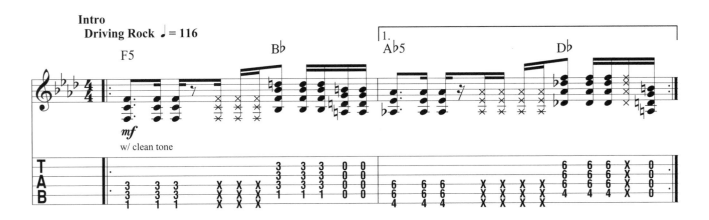

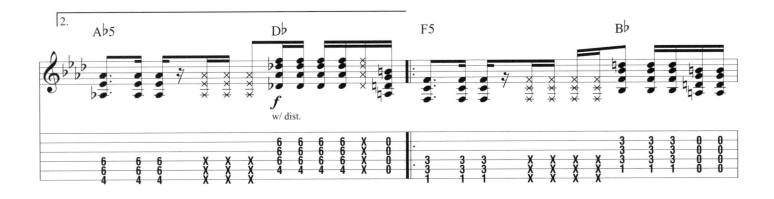

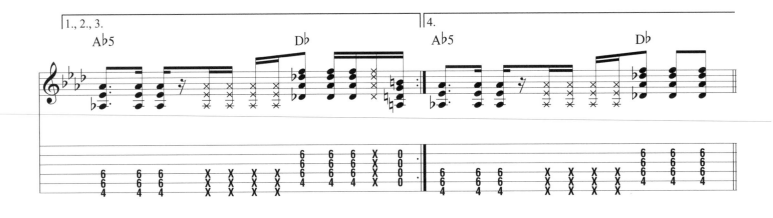

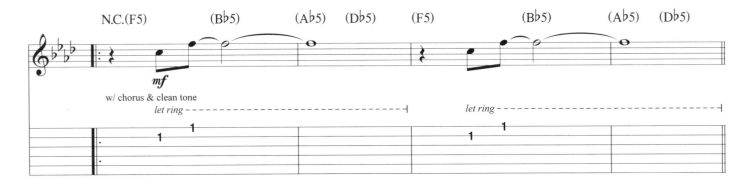

Copyright © 1991 The End Of Music, Primary Wave Tunes, M.J. Twelve Music and Murky Slough Music
All Rights for The End Of Music and Primary Wave Tunes Administered by BMG Rights Management (US) LLC
All Rights Reserved   Used by Permission

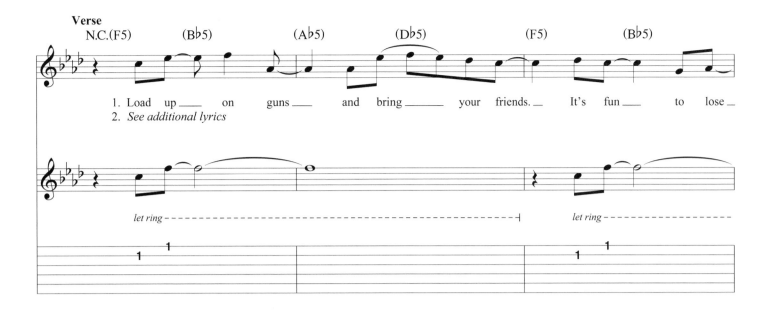

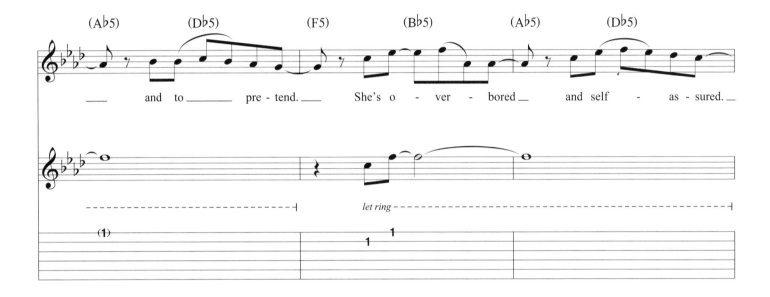

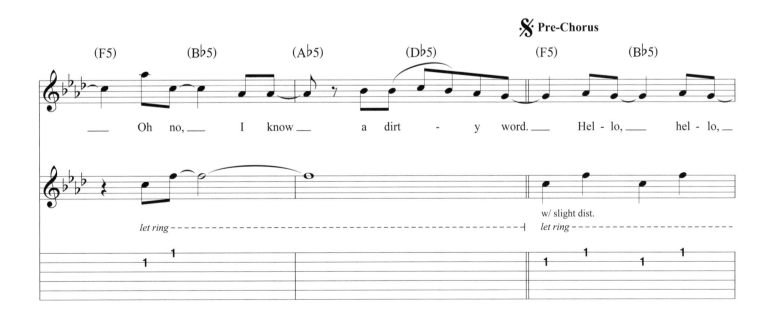

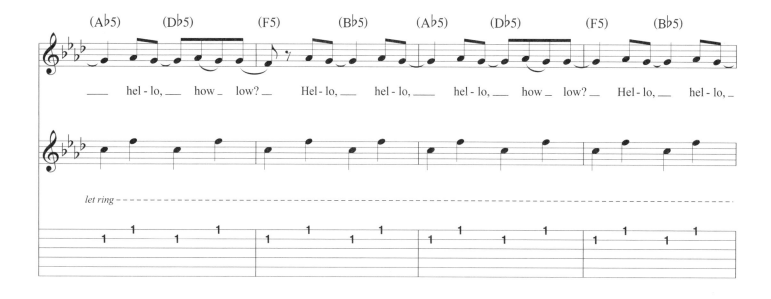

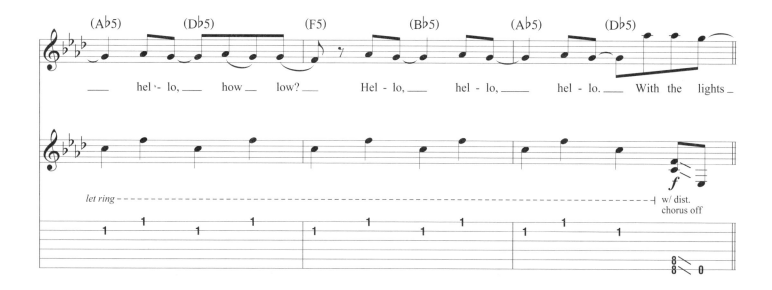

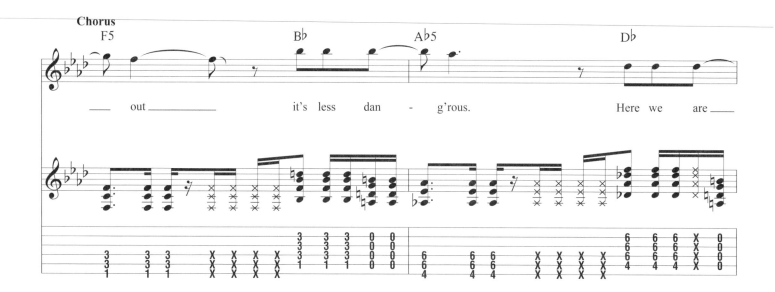

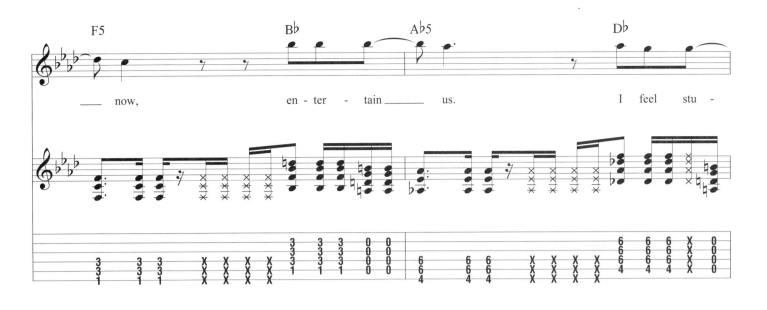

now, en - ter - tain   us.   I feel stu -

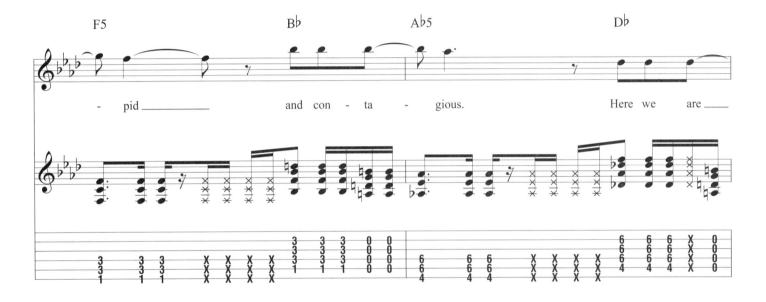

- pid   and con - ta - gious.   Here we are

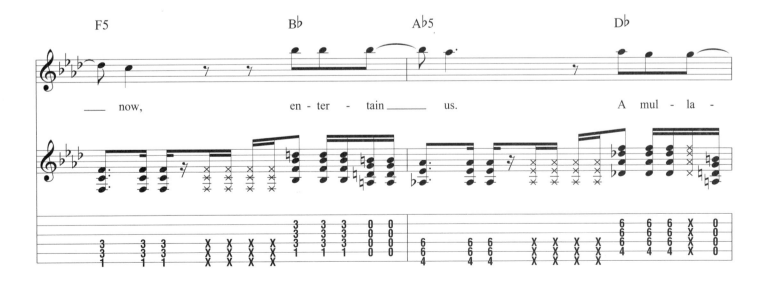

now, en - ter - tain   us.   A mul - la -

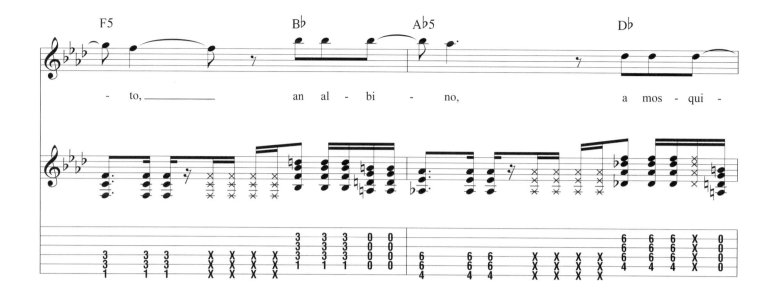

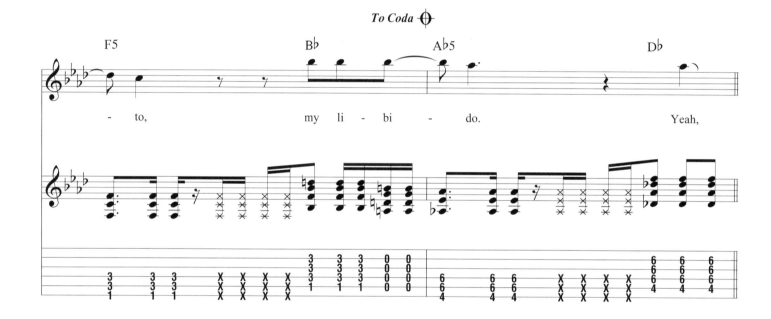

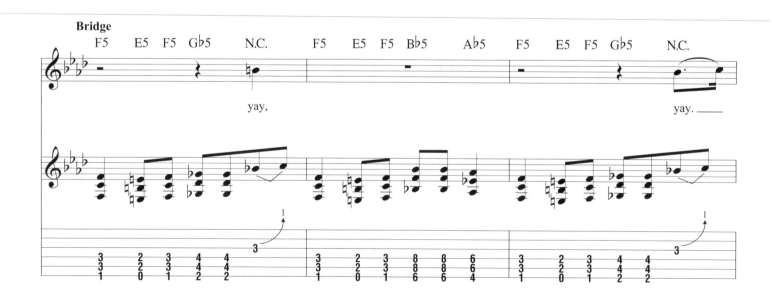

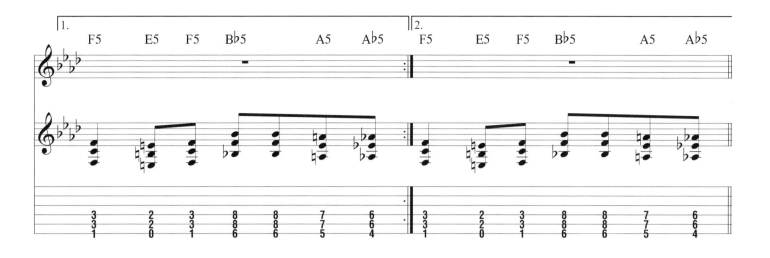

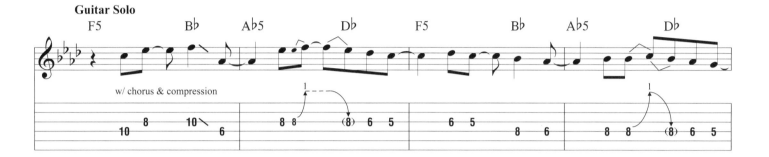

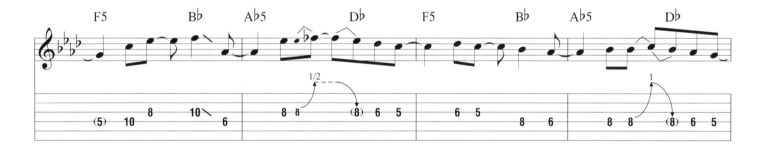

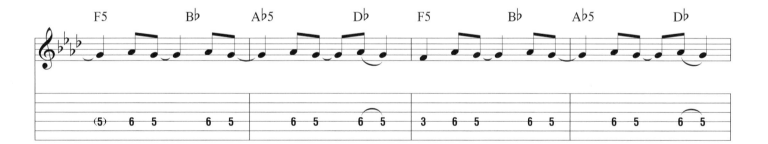

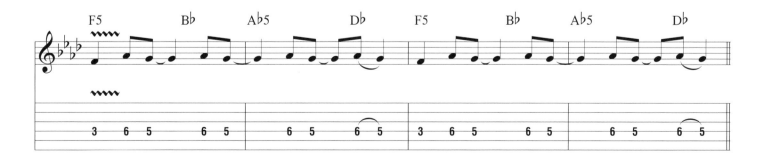

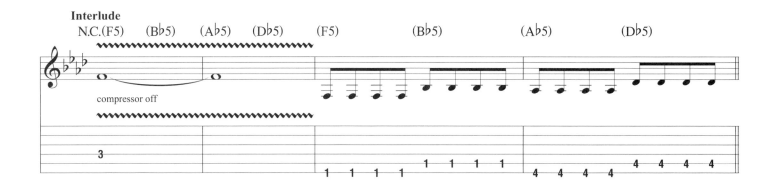

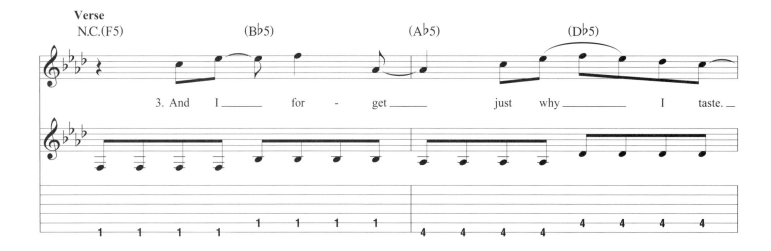

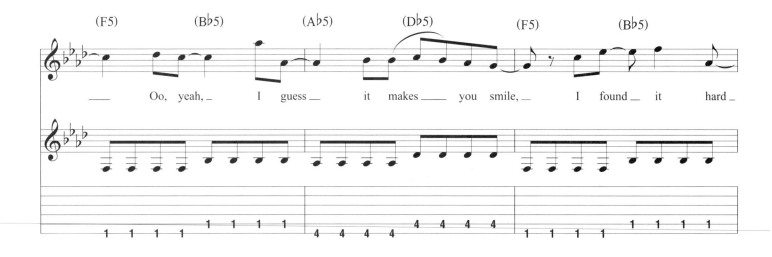

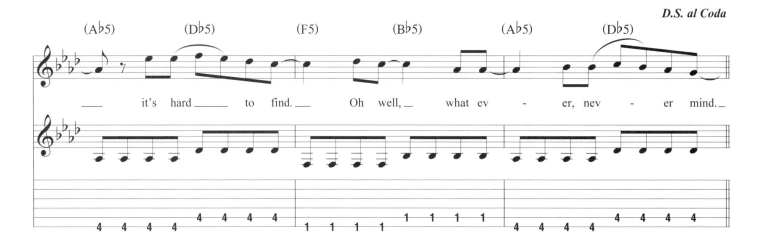

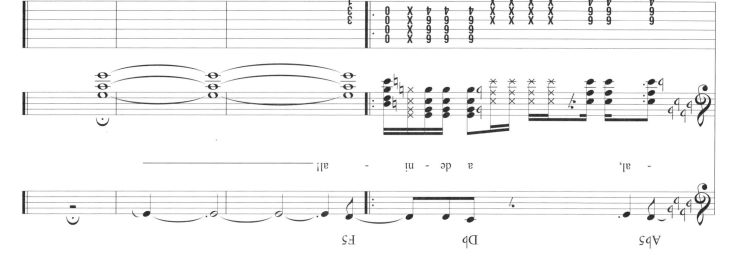

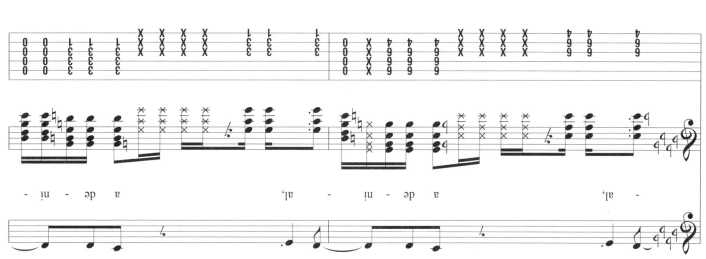

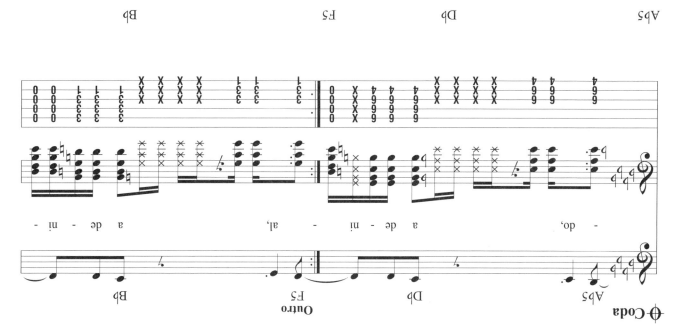

Additional Lyrics

2. I'm worse at what I do best,
And for this gift I feel blessed.
Our little group has always been
And always will until the end.

GUITAR NOTATION LEGEND

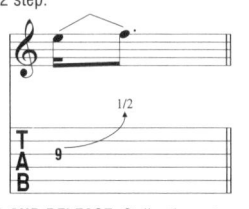

THE MUSICAL STAFF shows pitches and rhythms and is divided by bar lines into measures. Pitches are named after the first seven letters of the alphabet.

TABLATURE graphically represents the guitar fingerboard. Each horizontal line represents a string, and each number represents a fret.

4th string, 2nd fret

1st & 2nd strings open, played together

open D chord

HALF-STEP BEND: Strike the note and bend up 1/2 step.

WHOLE-STEP BEND: Strike the note and bend up one step.

GRACE NOTE BEND: Strike the note and immediately bend up as indicated.

SLIGHT (MICROTONE) BEND: Strike the note and bend up 1/4 step.

BEND AND RELEASE: Strike the note and bend up as indicated, then release back to the original note. Only the first note is struck.

PRE-BEND: Bend the note as indicated, then strike it.

VIBRATO: The string is vibrated by rapidly bending and releasing the note with the fretting hand.

PALM MUTING: The note is partially muted by the pick hand lightly touching the string(s) just before the bridge.

P.M.

HAMMER-ON: Strike the first (lower) note with one finger, then sound the higher note (on the same string) with another finger by fretting it without picking.

PULL-OFF: Place both fingers on the notes to be sounded. Strike the first note and without picking, pull the finger off to sound the second (lower) note.

LEGATO SLIDE: Strike the first note and then slide the same fret-hand finger up or down to the second note. The second note is not struck.

SHIFT SLIDE: Same as legato slide, except the second note is struck.

TRILL: Very rapidly alternate between the notes indicated by continuously hammering on and pulling off.

TAPPING: Hammer ("tap") the fret indicated with the pick-hand index or middle finger and pull off to the note fretted by the fret hand.

NATURAL HARMONIC: Strike the note while the fret-hand lightly touches the string directly over the fret indicated.

Harm.

PINCH HARMONIC: The note is fretted normally and a harmonic is produced by adding the edge of the thumb or the tip of the index finger of the pick hand to the normal pick attack.

P.H.

TREMOLO PICKING: The note is picked as rapidly and continuously as possible.

VIBRATO BAR DIVE AND RETURN: The pitch of the note or chord is dropped a specified number of steps (in rhythm), then returned to the original pitch.

w/ bar

VIBRATO BAR SCOOP: Depress the bar just before striking the note, then quickly release the bar.

w/ bar

VIBRATO BAR DIP: Strike the note and then immediately drop a specified number of steps, then release back to the original pitch.

w/ bar

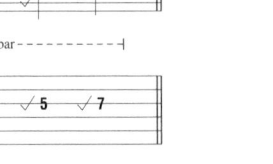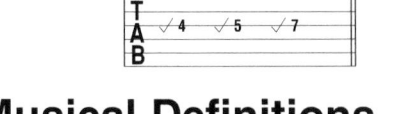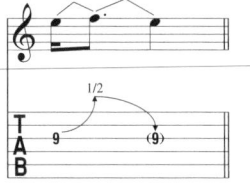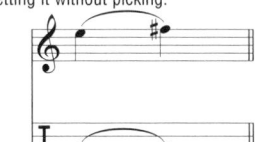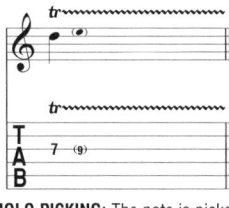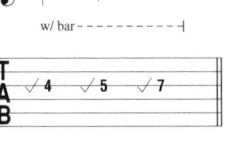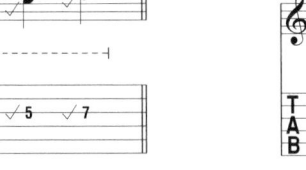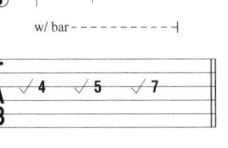

Additional Musical Definitions

(accent) • Accentuate note (play it louder).

(staccato) • Play the note short.

D.S. al Coda • Go back to the sign (𝄋), then play until the measure marked "***To Coda***," then skip to the section labelled "**Coda**."

D.C. al Fine • Go back to the beginning of the song and play until the measure marked "***Fine***" (end).

Fill • Label used to identify a brief melodic figure which is to be inserted into the arrangement.

N.C. • Harmony is implied.

 • Repeat measures between signs.

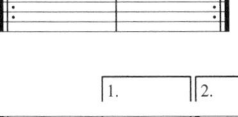 • When a repeated section has different endings, play the first ending only the first time and the second ending only the second time.